Moth

Animal

Series editor: Jonathan Burt

Moth

Matthew Gandy

REAKTION BOOKS

For my parents, Maggie and Mike

Published by
REAKTION BOOKS LTD
Unit 32, Waterside
44–48 Wharf Road
London N1 7UX, UK
www.reaktionbooks.co.uk

First published 2016, reprinted 2017
Copyright © Matthew Gandy 2016

Printed and bound in China by 1010 Printing International Ltd

A catalogue record for this book is available from the British Library

ISBN 978 1 78023 585 1

Contents

1 Multitudes

Ea quae scimus sunt pars minima eorum quae ignoramus. (The ones we know form only a fraction of the many of which we have no knowledge.)
Carl Linnaeus[1]

Most of us, said Austerlitz, know nothing of moths except that they eat holes in carpets and clothes and have to be kept at bay by the use of camphor and naphthalene, although in truth their lineage is among the most ancient and most remarkable in the whole history of nature.
W. G. Sebald[2]

Unlike their gaudy day-flying cousins, moths seem to reside in the shadows, denizens of the night circling around streetlights or caught momentarily in the glare of car headlights on a country lane. If butterflies have become a metaphor for graceful exhibitionism, gliding effortlessly between flowers or basking in bright sunshine, moths have too often been relegated to a realm of darkness and mystery. As for closer encounters with moths, like those to which W. G. Sebald alludes, these are more likely to be the dismay at finding a favourite sweater reduced to a kind of woollen version of Emmental cheese.

The idea that butterflies and moths are related yet opposites is somewhat artificial. For a start, there are many more species of day-flying moths than there are butterflies, and as for colours and patterns, many moths rival or even exceed butterflies in the dazzling range of their markings. In taxonomic terms, there is no substantive distinction between moths and butterflies as they are grouped together under the insect order Lepidoptera, a term first used by the Swedish naturalist Carl Linnaeus in 1735. It derives from the Greek words λεπίς (*lepís*), meaning 'scale', and πτερόν (*pterón*), meaning 'wing', because their wings are covered by thousands of

Centre-barred Sallow, *Atethmia centrago*, photographed in Stoke Newington, London.

The strikingly marked Magpie Moth, *Abraxas grossulariata*, was known to both Aristotle and Pliny.

tiny scales which produce the striking array of different colours, patterns and visual effects.[3] These are the 'mealy wings' that Achilles mentions in William Shakespeare's *Troilus and Cressida*, because of the powdery texture of dislodged scales.[4]

The order Lepidoptera comprises over 174,000 currently described species, making up about 7 per cent of all known life on Earth.[5] Only three other insect orders are as species-rich as the Lepidoptera: Hymenoptera (bees, wasps and ants), Diptera (flies) and, most numerous of all, Coleoptera (beetles), which currently includes one in six of all known species.[6] The order Lepidoptera is divided at present into 126 families, of which only six are considered butterflies. To put this another way, there are about 18,000 species of butterflies in the order – just under 10 per cent of the total – while the rest are moths. However, only a proportion of the total species have been classified, so the real or 'extant' number of species is likely to be far greater. Some estimates suggest that

8

there may be around half a million species in the order with the majority of new discoveries likely to be derived from the under-studied realm of moths. It is moths that continue to make up a significant part of what the biologist Edward O. Wilson terms the 'blank spaces on the biodiversity map', with over 800 new species of Lepidoptera described in scientific journals every year.[7]

Despite cultural assumptions about the differences between moths and butterflies, this scientific conundrum has perplexed taxonomists for centuries. Linnaeus, for example, used only a rudimentary range of morphological features and suggested the two could be distinguished by the shape of the wings when the insects were at rest. A few decades later, the French zoologist Pierre André Latreille (1762–1833) introduced a division between day-flying and night-flying species, which he termed the *diurni* and *nocturni*, yet there are many butterflies, especially in the tropics, which are partially nocturnal, as well as familiar migratory species such as the Monarch, *Danaus plexippus*, or Red Admiral, *Vanessa atalanta*, that will fly at night in order to cover long distances.[8] The French botanist and lepidopterist Jean Baptiste Boisduval (1799–1879) suggested that the shape of antennae could be used, distinguishing the club-tipped antennae of butterflies, which he named the Rhopalocera, from everything else, which he gathered under the miscellaneous category of the Heterocera.[9] In this sense Boisduval followed earlier observers of moths such as the English naturalist Moses Harris (1730–*c*. 1788), who stated that 'the Horns or Antenna of a Butterfly, hath a Knob, or Ball at the Extremity or End of each, and are for the most Part pretty straight' whereas 'the Antenna of Moths, chiefly diminish gradually, and end in a sharp Point'.[10] These debates on the differences between butterflies and moths seem to have been very much European in origin: in Japan, for example, the attempt to differentiate moths from butterflies only strongly emerged with the growth of European cultural and scientific influence (especially in the post-Edo era after 1867).[11]

Current scientific debates continue to highlight the taxonomic ambiguity of the distinction between moths and butterflies. Of the six Lepidoptera families regarded as butterflies, two are somewhat intermediate in form: the Hesperiidae, including the skippers and their allies, which lack clubbed antennae (they are known as 'skippers' because of their skittish mode of flight); and the Hedylidae, a small group of partially nocturnal insects restricted to Central and Latin America that were formerly considered moths but have recently been reclassified as butterflies. Additionally, many day-flying moths in the Uraniidae family, such as the Madagascan Sunset Moth, *Chrysiridia rhipheus*, bear a striking resemblance to butterflies, with their spectacular tails and shimmering array of colours.

The Madagascan Sunset Moth, *Chrysiridia rhipheus*, was initially believed to be a butterfly but was later reclassified as a moth.

Of the 120 or so families that are definitively regarded as moths, the most species-rich are the Noctuidae, the Geometridae and the so-called 'superfamily' Pyraloidea. The rather thick-bodied Noctuidae, widely referred to as 'owlets', have recently been extended by some taxonomists to include tiger moths, tussock moths and others, as part of a new 'superfamily'.[12] The Geometridae, by contrast, are often delicate and beautifully patterned moths that typically rest with their camouflaged wings held flat against bark, leaves or rocks. They are widely known as 'loopers' or 'inch worms' because as caterpillars they move by making an inverted U-shape, owing to the fact that they possess only one pair of prolegs for walking rather than the usual four (the family name is derived from the Greek word μέτρηση, *metrisi*, meaning 'measurement'). The vast Pyraloidea superfamily, now divided into the Pyralidae and Crambidae, contains a wide diversity of species, including some aquatic caterpillars and many taxa yet to be described. The Crambidae, for example, include the many 'grass moths' – small

Phaiogramma faustinaria is one of many green-coloured Geometridae species whose vibrant colours quickly fade to dull yellow in insect collections. This specimen was found in Almería, Spain.

The Luna Moth, *Actias luna*, is found in North America, and lives for only a few days because it does not feed.

species that fly up from almost any meadow or patch of rough grass – along with recently discovered spider mimics that have curious leg-like markings across their wings.

Another distinctive family, the Sphingidae, includes the fast-flying hawk-moths, which often play a significant role in plant pollination. Other families are the Saturniidae, with many of the most spectacular species yet described, such as the atlas and moon moths; the Bombycidae, which includes the domesticated silk moth; the Notodontidae, which consists of the prominents (named after their distinctive wing tufts) and kittens (so-called because of the kitten-like silhouette-shapes on the back of their caterpillars); the Sesiidae, a remarkable assemblage of wasp mimics that do not look like moths at all; the Limacodidae, or slug moths, which includes some of the most bizarre caterpillars yet encountered, with elongated spines and other strange protuberances; and the Zygaenidae, a distinctive group of often brightly coloured and highly poisonous day-flying moths. Some other families are perhaps best known simply as pests, such as the Tortricidae, especially those whose larvae damage fruit, and the Tineidae, including 'clothes moths' and other species that can digest keratin (a fibrous protein found in hair, skin and other organic matter).

With wingspans ranging in size from a few millimetres to nearly 30 cm (12 in.), moths display an extraordinary diversity in size and shape. Among the smallest moths are many so-called leaf miners

This wasp mimic, *Synanthedon codeti*, from the Sesiidae family, is found in south-west Europe and its caterpillars develop inside the branches of oak trees.

The Atlas Moth, *Attacus atlas*, is one of the world's largest moths. In addition to being a source of silk it is also an inspiration for the fictional Japanese monster Mothra. This photograph was taken in the botanical garden at Masaryk University, Brno, Czech Republic.

– especially from the families Gracillariidae and Nepticulidae – whose caterpillars live most of their lives inside leaves, producing intricate galleries or mines as they discreetly nibble their way under the protective cuticles of plants. These tiny moths are easily overlooked by even experienced entomologists, and their presence is often best detected by these mines and other traces left by their larvae. By contrast, the Saturniidae includes many of the world's largest insects. The strikingly marked Atlas Moth, *Attacus atlas*, from Southeast Asia, often has a wingspan of over 25 cm (10 in.), while an even bigger wingspan of nearly 30 cm (12 in.) has been recorded for the Noctuid moth *Thysania agrippina*, known as the White Witch or Birdwing Moth, found in Central and Latin America.

This striking divergence in wingspan has led to attempts to classify moths by size on the basis of assumptions about their evolutionary sophistication. Nineteenth-century scientists consequently suggested a division between Macrolepidoptera and Microlepidoptera – or 'Macros' and 'Micros'. However, this distinction is replete with anomalies. The 'primitive' Hepialidae, for example, which includes ghost moths, swift moths and their allies, are classified as 'Micros', yet the family also includes some very large species, especially in the Australasian ecozone. The more 'advanced' Noctuidae are regarded as 'Macros', but the family includes some very small species that have often been mistaken for 'Micros'.

One of the most distinctive features of the Lepidoptera is their life cycle, in particular their dramatic ability to undergo metamorphosis from a crawling caterpillar into a winged insect with almost no physical resemblance to its earlier life stages. A perennial focus

The tiny but brightly coloured *Oecophora bractella* – one of the Microlepidoptera – is associated with old deciduous woodlands, and its caterpillars feed on rotten wood and fungi.

of fascination, metamorphosis has long been a rich source of cultural symbolism. In his *Divine Comedy*, the Italian poet Dante Alighieri (1265–1321) compares the physical metamorphosis of insects to a spiritual transformation:

> O proud Christians, weary wretches, who, weak
> in mental vision, put your faith in backward steps,
> do you not perceive that we are worms born to
> form the angelic butterfly that flies to justice
> without a shield?
> Why is it that your spirit floats on high, since you
> are like defective insects, like worms in whom formation is
> lacking?[13]

In Dante's vision of spiritual redemption, it is the day-flying butterfly that survives the fire, rather than the nocturnal moth that is consumed by flames, although they both originate from 'worms'.[14] In this sense, therefore, metamorphosis is conceived as a process of divine selection in the afterlife. Dante's distinction is also hinted at in the oft-quoted aphorism of the Italian novelist Giovanni Papini (1881–1956), who writes: 'The moth is in love with what the tiger fears. But humankind – a wild beast destined to become an angelic butterfly – is at the same time stunned and attracted by the fire.'[15]

Before the rapid development of the experimental sciences in the seventeenth century, the ability of butterflies and moths to produce another generation of larvae via eggs was unknown. Caterpillars, along with other worm-like creatures, were instead believed to be produced through a process of spontaneous generation: Aristotle, for example, thought that they simply emerged out of green leaves from 'dew condensed by the sun'.[16] The Roman naturalist Pliny the Elder similarly believed that 'some creatures are generated from rain in the earth'.[17] Pliny was also familiar with the hircine caterpillars of the Goat Moth, *Cossus cossus* (so-called because its larvae smell of goats), which he believed had simply emerged out of the wood on which they feed.

The metamorphosis of moths and butterflies involves four stages: egg (ovum), caterpillar (larva), chrysalis (pupa) and adult (imago). The eggs are the first stage in this transformation, and the fact that they are laid in their hundreds indicates that the few individuals that finally emerge as adults represent a marvel of survival as well as morphogenesis. Most moth larvae are 'phytophagous', or plant eating, and they are perhaps best conceived as a kind of specialized eating machine locked in a sophisticated evolutionary combat with plant defence systems. While plants have evolved to produce a variety of chemicals to ward off the hungry hordes of caterpillars and other insects, some caterpillars have developed the ability to chew on specific leaf veins to limit the flow of these resins and saps. Other species possess a sophisticated digestive system capable of breaking down woody plant tissues, and even of sequestering highly toxic chemicals to use against would-be predators or for the production of pheromones. Plant defence chemicals, which range from opiates to rubber, have proved of immense value throughout human history because of their medicinal, culinary or material properties. Tannins, for example, which are so vital to viticulture, are in fact digestibility inhibitors that help protect plants from caterpillars and other insects. To enjoy a glass of wine, then, is to experience the co-evolutionary complexity of plants and insects.[18]

Caterpillars share a few basic features: they have a head with rudimentary eyes, a spinneret for the extrusion of silk, and bodies with a series of respiratory pores called spiracles. Beyond these basic anatomical features, however, there is a stunning diversity in their morphological structures and behavioural adaptations. Because the caterpillar is likely to increase its mass by at least 1,000 times after hatching, it must periodically shed its outer skin via a series of moults that are interspersed with growth phases called 'instars'. Though five or six instars are typical, there are some caterpillars that undergo eight or nine (such as the 'slug caterpillars' of the family Limacodidae). This growth phase can vary considerably in length between species, and can even last years in very cold or inhospitable environments.[19]

When the caterpillar is ready to pupate, it often undergoes a series of changes: it may lose weight, change colour or begin to behave differently – for example, by wandering long distances. In many cases the caterpillar forms a protective cocoon before it undergoes its final moult. In some species this may be located above ground, in others it is buried in earth or leaf litter, while others attach themselves to plants or other substrates by a set of hooks called the cremaster, sometimes with an added silken girdle for stability. Inside the pupa, the caterpillar begins a remarkable series of changes, commencing by effectively dissolving its own flesh. The energy released is then used to produce a completely new set of organs, including antennae, compound eyes, jointed legs, reproductive organs and wings (except for those species that have wingless females).[20] Although the pupal stage normally lasts anywhere between a week and a few months, there are some species that will wait a couple of years before final emergence: in the case of bogus yucca moths of the genus *Prodoxus* from the American Southwest, adults have been recorded emerging more than 30 years after pupation.[21]

Adults are very vulnerable on emergence since their soft and crumpled wings must be rapidly expanded and dried to enable flight. In addition to their distinctive scale-covered wings, moths possess a range of precise physiological adaptations to help them locate food, find a mate and avoid predators. Their compound eyes comprise thousands of individual 'eye units' called ommatidia. In many species, these are specially adapted for nocturnal vision and can detect colours on the ultraviolet end of the spectrum that are invisible to the human eye. At night, moth eyes can resemble 'glowing coals' when fluttering at an illuminated windowpane or caught in the beam of a torch. The phenomenon is caused by a reflective layer (termed the *tapetum lucidum*), located behind each of the tiny receptors in the ommatidia, that serves to increase the ability of each photoreceptor to capture light.[22] The striking, if disconcerting, sight of gleaming eyes is reputedly the origin of the name 'owlets' in North America for the family Noctuidae (also called *Eulen* – owls – in German-speaking countries).

Many moths also have sophisticated tympanal (hearing) organs that in some cases are specifically adapted to detect the echolocation calls of bats (their main nocturnal predators). On hearing a bat, some species will fly in the opposite direction, adopt an erratic flight pattern or even dive to the ground to avoid danger. Other species are able to produce sounds that confuse bats and other predators, and which may also serve to communicate with other moths (as in the courtship behaviour of some tiger moths).[23]

A distinctive feature of the Lepidoptera is the structure of the proboscis used for drinking nectar, water or other liquids. Its size and shape vary between species, according to their food source, and there are also some moths that lack a proboscis and do not feed at all, such as many types of silk moths. The Death's-head Hawk-moth, *Acherontia atropos*, has a stumpy proboscis specially adapted for stealing honey from beehives (hence one of its earlier vernacular names, 'bee robber'). Others possess a sharp proboscis that can puncture the skin of fruit, and in one group – the vampire moths from the genus *Calyptra* of the Noctuidae family – this has evolved into a barb-like structure that enables them to pierce through skin and drink mammalian blood (the Swiss scientist Hans Bänziger, the leading specialist who works on this group of moths,

Europe's largest moth, the Great Peacock Moth, *Saturnia pyri*, was the focus of pioneering experiments by Jean-Henri Fabre into insect communication by pheromones.

Vincent Van Gogh, *Great Peacock Moth* (1889). Van Gogh's painting provides a contrast with the increasing emphasis on more narrowly taxonomic forms of entomological illustration in the late 19th century.

has even used his own hand as a laboratory to prove their feeding habits). Although vampire moths are not thought to carry any diseases – unlike mosquitoes – their northward spread from southern Europe due to climate change has provoked mild alarm in Finland and Sweden.

With the exception of moth families that have the earliest evolutionary origins, such as the Eriocraniidae and Micropterigidae, most species have elaborate, multisensory antennae. In many species the male antennae serve as feathery olfactory organs. Their shape increases their surface area, producing a highly sensitive organ that is capable of detecting a few molecules of scent produced by a female from several kilometres away. The Saturniidae (including the atlas, emperor and many silk moths) make use of these organs in sophisticated courtship patterns based around the use of pheromones. The French entomologist Jean-Henri Fabre (1823–1915) was among the first scientists to observe this directly. In his memoirs he recounts placing a freshly emerged female specimen

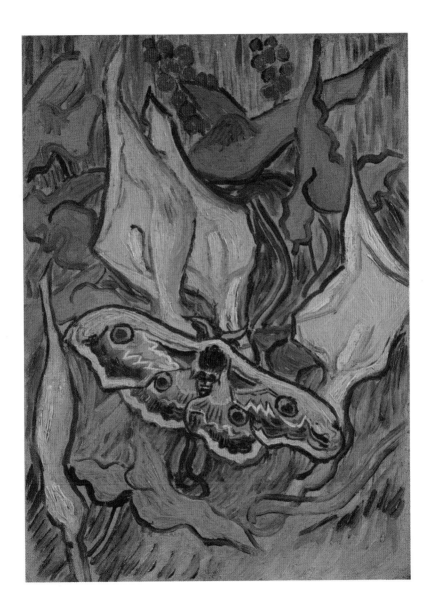

Jean-Henri Fabre photographed by Félix Nadar (1880). Fabre was an acute observer of insect behaviour and a significant influence on vitalist philosophies of nature.

of Europe's largest moth, the Great Peacock Moth, *Saturnia pyri*, in a 'wire-gauze bell jar' in his study. Later that day, as his family were going to bed, his young son suddenly began to shout with excitement:

'Come quick!' he screams. 'Come and see these moths, big as birds! The room is full of them!' I hurry in. There is enough to justify the child's enthusiastic and hyperbolical exclamations, an invasion as yet unprecedented in our house, a raid of giant Moths.[24]

In all, Fabre counted over 40 male moths that had entered the house. Unable to explain the extraordinary scene, he wondered whether moths had some hidden means of communication, a 'wireless telegraphy' analogous to the recently discovered Hertzian radio waves.[25] We now know the mechanism behind this signalling: in order to attract a mate, the female releases a small amount of pheromones from her body at a precise moment that will ensure the chemicals are carried downwind. In a further twist to this olfactory choreography, closely related species of silk moths release pheromones at different times so that their courtship is staggered through the night.[26] Though the precise chemical compounds for many species have yet to be identified, scientists are able to use synthetically produced pheromones to monitor pest species and also to record highly elusive species such as the wasp-mimicking Sesiidae, whose presence can sometimes only be revealed by chemical lures. However, the remarkable ability of moths to communicate with each other over vast distances perpetuates a sense of mystery even today, despite our greater awareness of this natural chemistry; in Dario Argento's cult horror film *Profondo Rosso* (1975), this ability is attributed to telepathic powers. The film's main protagonist is engaged in research into the communicative power of insects (a theme Argento returns to in his later film *Phenomena* of 1985). The effects of moth pheromones are also used as a metaphor for human attraction in Barbara Kingsolver's novel *Prodigal Summer* (2000), where she explores intricate patterns of human and non-human interaction on an Appalachian mountainside.

How long have moths existed on earth? There are very few fossil records for Lepidoptera because their fragile wings have left little trace, unlike other insects such as beetles whose remains are an important source of data for the reconstruction of past environments. Occasional complete moth or butterfly fossils have been found in a relatively well-preserved state, but only where special circumstances such as falling volcanic ash have forced living insects to the ground and then quickly formed a protective layer over their intact bodies. The evidence we possess suggests that the Lepidoptera emerged later than other insect orders such as Odonata (dragonflies), Orthoptera (grasshoppers) and Coleoptera (beetles). The oldest fossil record of a winged insect similar to a butterfly or moth has been dated to the Lower Jurassic era, some 190 million years ago, but the first definitive example of a moth fossil dates from the Lower Cretaceous era, between 146 and 100 million years ago. Additionally, possible examples of leaf mines (the tiny galleries produced by some caterpillars) have been discovered in fossils from the Mid-Cretaceous Dakota Formation, dating from 100 million years ago.

From the Cretaceous period onwards the fossil presence of Lepidoptera becomes more frequent, with especially rich assemblages found in the Baltic amber deposits of the Eocene epoch around 56 million years ago and the Oligocene epoch from about 34 million years ago.[27] The fossil record suggests that the Cretaceous era also saw increasing diversification of moth species, associated with the rise of flowering plants on which most of their caterpillars feed.[28] Insects and plants form part of a complex co-evolutionary dynamic since many flowering plants rely on insects – principally bees, but

Global bio-diversity can be divided into a series of ecozones within which the neotropics of Central and Latin America have the greatest number of Lepidoptera species.

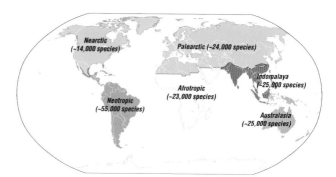

New developments in geographic information systems (GIS) and conservation biology have enabled the development of more accurate cartographic approaches to the identification of biodiversity hotspots: note the concentration of total species richness in the Amazon basin and the Andes.

also occasionally moths – for pollination. Other critical clues for the origin of some moth species are provided by their co-evolutionary relationship with bats as their main nocturnal predators. Since bats do not appear until the Early Tertiary era some 50 to 60 million years ago, we can assume that many of the most species-rich moth families, such as the Geometridae and the Noctuidae with their specialized hearing organs for avoiding bats, must also have begun to evolve at this time.

Today there remain significant differences in the global distribution of biodiversity when it comes to moths. The World Wide

Fund for Nature (WWF) currently divides the earth into a series of eight biogeographical zones, or 'ecozones', and all of these, with the exception of Oceania (the Fijian Islands, Micronesia and Polynesia, excluding New Zealand) and the Antarctic, harbour a bewildering diversity of Lepidoptera. The greatest number of species is found in the Neotropic ecozone, which includes South America, Central America, the Caribbean and part of Florida (some 55,000 to date). Recent research into moth distribution patterns reveals that the global 'hotspots' for biodiversity are not in the lowland Amazon basin, as has been widely assumed, but further east in the higher altitude rainforests of southern Ecuador and Peru.[29] The other key concentration of biodiversity for Lepidoptera lies in the zone extending from Papua New Guinea, Indonesia and Malaysia to Bhutan, which is significantly under-researched: according to the entomologist John B. Heppner, writing over twenty years ago, the 'vast' moth fauna of New Guinea 'has hardly been touched'.[30]

The Sapphire-tailed Clearwing, *Loxophlebia nomia*, is a neo-tropical wasp or firefly mimic closely related to the tiger moths.

Acraga moorei is a member of the Dalceridae family from the Andes, a region now recognized as the most important global biodiversity hotspot for moths. This specimen was found in the Manu Cloud Forest of Peru.

Why has such immense biodiversity evolved? How can so many closely related species coexist? It may partly be explained by the huge range of co-evolutionary relationships with plants on which most moths feed in the larval stage: an individual plant can support an immense range of different species, not just through its leaves but through the provision of micro-niches by roots, stems, galls or even woody tissue under bark. Accumulations of dead or withered leaves also provide additional food sources for caterpillars living in the rich leaf litter that accumulates on the forest floor, as do the enormous range of fungi that grow in association with plants at different stages of their life cycle. While some species remain relatively generalist, surviving on a range of plants and other food sources across a variety of environmental and climatic conditions, others are highly specialist, dependent on one type of plant for survival. With the greater diversity of plant species in ecosystems such as rainforests, the total number of moth species rises although the relative balance between 'generalist' and 'specialist' species still remains

The rarely photographed *Trosia dimas* is also found in Peru.

a matter of scientific conjecture. If we add in variations in altitude, and yet more ecological niches, there is probably a further doubling in species abundance, which helps to explain why the Andes has become recognized as the undisputed global hotspot for Lepidoptera biodiversity.

Moths appear to possess an evolutionary dynamism that has allowed them to adapt to a very wide range of conditions, including some surprisingly cold environments. While many species from temperate latitudes survive the harshest months of winter in the egg stage, with the caterpillars eventually hatching in the spring, there are exceptions such as the Winter Moth, *Operophtera brumata*, which produces its own kind of antifreeze to remain active at low temperatures. In Greenland and parts of northern Canada, the Arctic

The geometrid *Pantherodes pardalaria* photographed in Brazil.

Caterpillar of the Artic Woolly Bear Moth survives extreme conditions by altering its own body structure and producing glycerol as a kind of antifreeze.

Woolly Bear Moth, *Gynaephora groenlandica*, spends several years as a caterpillar, during which it may be frozen solid an astonishing 90 per cent of the time in temperatures as low as −70°C (−94°F).

Pressures from predation may also be a factor in promoting moth diversity. Moths form an integral 'building block' of ecological systems because their larvae consume huge quantities of biomass, including dead wood and fallen leaves, and they are themselves, at different stages in their life cycle, a key source of food for other animals such as birds, mammals, reptiles and other insects.[31]An insectivorous bat may consume up to half its own body weight in food each night. Moths have consequently developed ingenious and diverse ways of avoiding predators: for example, *Cydia deshaisiana*, found in Mexico and the American Southwest, develops as a caterpillar inside a seedpod for additional protection. Its habit of 'jumping' by bashing its head against the side of the pod so that it can change location and possibly evade seed-eating predators has earned it the vernacular name of the Mexican jumping bean (*frijoles saltarines*).[32] Other moths actually want to be eaten by predators in a sacrificial strategy: the female of some Psychidae species (also known as 'bag worms' because of their distinctive larval cases) is not only wingless but smooth and grub-like, and may fall to the ground and wiggle around to catch the attention of birds, thereby ensuring that its eggs are dispersed through bird droppings.[33] Intense pressure from predators may thus have increased bio-diversity by forcing moths to diversify their survival strategies at every stage of their life cycle; diversity itself can be seen as a form of defence, because there is such a bewildering variety of shapes and patterns for predators to contend with.[34] However, more beneficial and co-operative types of co-evolutionary relationships with other organisms have also developed. There are moths that live only in the fur of sloths, where the adult moths can survive on algae, sweat and other secretions, and also enjoy protection from avian predators:

the Tineid moth, *Cryptoses choloepi*, for example, lives exclusively in the fur of the Brown-throated Sloth, *Bradypus variegatus*, found in the forests of Central and South America.[35]

While migratory species are adept at colonizing new habitats, other families such as the delicately winged Geometridae are less mobile and more closely associated with specific ecosystems, such as broadleaf woodlands at temperate latitudes, or various types of rainforests or submontane forest habitats towards the equator.[36] Non-migratory species of tiger moths and their allies (subfamily Arctiinae) are also highly adapted to particular ecological niches: the caterpillars of some species eat lichens and other epiphytic plants that only grow under specific environmental conditions. We encounter an increasing number of such stenotopic species (those with narrow forms of niche specialization) at the later stages of ecological succession – the process of change over time – towards habitats such as forest ecosystems, where we can observe intricate forms of dynamic equilibrium: small disturbances such as the fall of an individual tree can allow a patchwork of light through the canopy, enabling a mosaic of ecological niches within a relatively stable larger structure.[37] Of particular interest to those in the field of conservation biology are the species with a highly restricted geographical distribution, a phenomenon that is referred to as endemicity. Geographical barriers such as mountain ranges and other complex topographies can enhance the rate of new species formation, not just by providing environmental variation, but by dividing populations so that small genetic differences can become more pronounced over time, until distinct species have diverged from a common ancestor.[38] Examples include closely related species occurring on different sides of the Pyrenees, with many endemic species of moths found in the Iberian Peninsula, whereas in Italy, by contrast, the north–south aligned mountain 'highway' has allowed easier movement with less speciation. One of the most dramatic examples of the effects of geographical isolation is in Hawaii, where several *Eupithecia* species of Geometrid moths have caterpillars that have taken up the evolutionary niche normally occupied by mantis-like predators: these entirely carnivorous larvae lurk among foliage and swing their bodies onto flies which they grab with their pincer-shaped front legs.

In some cases, the adaptability of moths can create problems; for example, where 'pest' species have exploited changing human lifestyles. Among the moths that have the most intimate relationship with people and their homes are the clothes moths of the Tineidae family. Many members of this family play a vital ecological role in breaking down some of the least biodegradable materials in nature, such as owl pellets or birds' nests. Yet some have a particular taste for fabrics (with a special fondness for wool), and their abundance is closely tied with aspects of human history including different types of clothes, heating and interior design. Formerly significant pests such as the Tapestry Moth, *Trichophaga tapetzella*, were already in decline in the early twentieth century, while other species such as *Tineola bisselliella* have recently become much more numerous. However, some Tineid moths also provide benefits, through their role in forensic entomology, for example, by helping to determine the age of a corpse: they only appear during the late stages of human decomposition, with their larvae consuming keratin and collagen contained in the dry remains of skin, hair, tendons and ligaments.[39]

There are pest species that can cause serious damage to crops or forests. Examples include the Gypsy Moth, *Lymantria dispar*, accidentally introduced into North America – as part of an ill-fated experiment in silk production during the 1860s – and capable of causing extensive defoliation. Conversely, some moths have been successfully used for biological pest control against invasive plants, as in Australia and Hawaii, since many species require specific foodplants for their caterpillars.[40] Pests of agricultural monocultures include the 'army worms' of the genus *Spodoptera* (family Noctuidae): these caterpillars move about at night in large numbers in search of food. On a smaller scale, orchard harvests are sometimes damaged by the larvae of the Codling Moth, *Cydia pomonella*, or 'apple worm', which originated in Europe but is now a significant pest across much of North America.

There are some species of moths that not only defoliate trees but form nests of caterpillars that shed irritating hairs. Although widespread in southern Europe, the Oak Processionary Moth, *Thaumetopoea processionea*, has recently spread northwards, provoking alarm in Belgium, the Netherlands and the UK – the caterpillars, which move in large 'processions', have hairs that can cause severe irritation, including bronchial infections. In the Korean Peninsula, there have been serious recent problems with deforestation by the Pine Moth, *Dendrolimus spectabilis*, which even led North Korea to seek emergency international assistance to help protect its forests (especially as the outbreak threatened landscapes near Pyongyang). Interestingly, a novel by the writer Yeo Jin, called the *Pine Caterpillar Moths That Ate Oak Leaves* (1987), uses the moth as a symbol of illegal logging in South Korea during the early 1960s under the Park Chung-hee military regime. In this instance, it is not caterpillars but political corruption that lies behind the destruction of forests.[41]

As this behavioural and evolutionary adaptability might suggest, moths and other insects respond rapidly to environmental change. This means that they can serve as highly sensitive indicators for tracking the ecological effects of climate change and other processes. The shifting patterns of insect distribution, including Lepidoptera, provide important evidence that climate change is already underway. In the UK, for example, increasing numbers of moths from central and southern Europe have been turning up, including many species never encountered before. Across Europe there is evidence of species extending their range either northwards or into higher altitude zones. Europe also retains a montane archipelago of relict faunas that are now under threat from warmer temperatures: while some species that prefer cooler environments can retreat northwards, others are effectively trapped, with their increasingly fragmented and isolated populations left with nowhere to go. Similarly, climate change has been associated in North America with changes in moth distribution and abundance, which has led to serious defoliation of woodlands.[42]

Although the recent decline in bees has attracted widespread attention, there is also evidence of parallel falls in the number of moths, butterflies and many other invertebrates. A recent study in the UK found that the total abundance of moths had fallen by about 28 per cent over a 40-year period, with an even greater decline in the south of Britain: an analysis of 337 common or widespread

The Spanish Moon Moth, *Actias isabellae*. An elusive and mysterious mountain species that has long been a source of entomological fascination and is on the IUCN Red List of Threatened Species.

34

The Argent and Sable, *Rheumaptera hastata*, has a dappled wing pattern not unlike sunlight falling through leaves. This specimen was found in Estonia.

species found that two-thirds of these had declined.[43] These findings are provided by the Rothamsted Insect Survey, which involves a network of over 400 light traps operated across Britain, coordinated from the Rothamsted research centre, first established in 1843 as an agricultural research station north of London. Another major long-term study of moths in Hungary – the 'Hungarian light trap network', in operation since the late 1950s – has also recorded a significant decline in both total abundance and species diversity over a 50-year period.[44] Other individual studies mirror these national findings: Jennifer Owen's remarkable 30-year study of moths in her own back garden in suburban Leicester reveals a similar decline since the early 1970s.[45]

Recent research on the remaining temperate forests of central Europe reveals very high levels of invertebrate biodiversity, but these types of niche ecosystems are now under increased threat from habitat destruction, including agricultural intensification, tourism (especially in alpine and coastal areas), urban sprawl (and increased levels of light pollution) and the clear-felling of ancient woodlands (as revealed by satellite imagery of Romania, Ukraine and elsewhere). As a result of these factors, many formerly common moth species of lowland Europe are now increasingly restricted to higher altitudes or less intensively cultivated areas.[46] Habitat fragmentation of this type has deleterious long-term effects on the viability of surviving populations. The declining genetic fitness of small and isolated populations, sometimes referred to as 'genetic drift', undermines the long-term capacity for survival. Many species of moths and butterflies exist as part of 'metapopulations' comprising multiple sites with fluctuating populations that periodically replenish each other, but with increasing distance between very small populations the extinction logic of genetic drift (as lower levels of genetic variety reduce the capacity for adaption) begins to set in.[47] Other factors across Europe and North America include the use of pesticides such as neonicotinoids, a class of neurotoxins known to affect bees but which has also been implicated in the decline of other invertebrates such as moths.[48]

These developments are worrying because moths play such a vital role in the wider functioning of ecosystems. For example, many species of migratory birds time their nesting season in northern Europe to coincide with the peak abundance of caterpillars. However, climate change is disrupting the ecology of these birds since they may arrive at higher latitudes only to find that the burst of spring caterpillar activity has already passed, leaving little food for them or their offspring.[49] Moth decline also has implications for plant pollination, because some 90 per cent of plants rely on insects for the spread of pollen. Studies in Costa Rica have found that hawk-moths (Sphingidae) are the main pollinators for about 10 per cent of the trees in some forests.[50] Furthermore, the larger and stronger flying species, such as hawk-moths, are able to 'outcross' flowers more easily by travelling longer distances than many other insects.[51]

Some plants are specially adapted for pollination by moths at night, with long-tubed corollas only accessible to the proboscis of a few species, or others may display a profusion of pale-coloured flowers that become highly fragrant at dusk. In the early 1860s Charles Darwin had become fascinated by a series of extremely long-spurred orchids from Madagascar, yet Darwin's supposition that these species must rely on very long-tongued hawk-moths for their pollination would have to wait for confirmation until sophisticated field observations were made in the 1990s.[52] The yucca plant, a genus containing about 50 species of trees and shrubs restricted to arid environments in the Americas, has developed a specialized relationship with moths of the Prodoxidae family, which use modified mouthparts to place pollen grains on the stigma of yucca flowers.[53] However, since very few moths have specialized organs for collecting pollen, their role is more likely to be that of 'accidental pollinators' through the dusting of their bodies while feeding.

It is not only adult moths, through their role in plant pollination, that are important for human well-being: caterpillars can serve as an important source of human nutrition. Larger caterpillars are widely eaten for food in Mexico, Africa and Southeast Asia.[54] Ethno-entomological studies of caterpillar consumption in sub-Saharan Africa have revealed that a wide variety of species are eaten, and that these form the basis of detailed local knowledge and extensive food classification systems.[55] In the Democratic Republic of Congo, for example, the consumption of some species for food, such as the Ngala, *Cirina forda*, and the Kaba, *Lobobunaea phaedusa*, has recently increased because of the expense or scarcity of other sources of protein.[56] The larvae of the Mopani, *Gonimbrasia belina*, which is a kind of silk moth, are a vital food source in Botswana, Zambia, Zimbabwe and other parts of southern Africa.[57] The 'mescal worm', or *gusano rojo*, found in tequila is actually a caterpillar, most often *Comadia redtenbacheri*, a member of the

Cossidae family, that bores into the agave plants from which the drink is distilled. The pupae of silk moths are also widely eaten in China, Japan, Thailand and elsewhere, especially since they perish anyway when their cocoons are used in sericulture. The cultivation of silkworms for food has even been suggested by recent Chinese researchers as a potential long-term source of protein for people living on space stations.[58] Given the high food-conversion efficiency of caterpillars compared with other types of food, such as beef or chicken, it is likely that insects will remain an important source of protein, possibly replacing meat altogether in science-fiction food scenarios.

Scientists warn that time is running out to complete the original Linnaean task of classifying all of nature, or even just half of it. Scores of species are being lost before they have ever been described, let alone studied for their potentially wider benefits or ecological significance. Almost any comprehensive survey of moths in less systematically studied parts of the planet turns up many new species. The ethical imperative to record and protect biodiversity, proselytized by scientists such as Daniel Janzen and Edward O. Wilson, resonates powerfully with wider environmental concerns over climate change, deforestation, pollution and other threats to both human survival and the natural world. Yet the dual ethical and scientific impetus behind the protection of biodiversity also harbours certain tensions about the implicit continuity of colonial patterns of knowledge production and the nature of interactions with those often impoverished or marginalized communities who inhabit the more remote locales where levels of biodiversity are highest and scientific knowledge most fragmentary or incomplete.[59] The rise of 'parataxonomy' in Costa Rica, for example, where villagers have been trained to collect, rear and then pickle caterpillars to contribute towards entomological research, poses complex ethical and political issues largely beyond the scope of existing taxonomic or scientific understanding. It is certainly the case that the remarkable insights from Costa Rica by Daniel Janzen and his colleagues could not have been completed without extensive local help, not just in terms of human labour, but from the indigenous knowledge. Recent award-winning publications have drawn on more than 28 years of collaboration between scientists and local parataxonomists, or *gusaneros* (derived from the Spanish word *gusano*, meaning caterpillar), who work at a series of caterpillar-rearing stations in the Área de Conservación Guanacaste in northwestern Costa Rica.[60]

Less contentious are the new 'citizen science' initiatives facilitated by the Internet. Specialist websites devoted to the study of moths receive hundreds of thousands of hits from the burgeoning realm of 'digital natural history', extending from bored security staff whose curiosity is transfixed by nocturnal insects flying around lights, to children discovering caterpillars and other traces of 'wild nature' in the middle of cities. Many cartographic projects could not be completed without the data provided by thousands of amateur enthusiasts, while long-term research into population fluctuations relies on the monitoring activities of dispersed networks of expertise. The distinction between amateurs and experts is blurry in the fields of ecology and insect systematics, with the main limiting factor often being time rather than access to expensive laboratory facilities.

Curiosity in the natural world is growing, even or perhaps especially in cities, and moths have formed part of this upsurge in popular science. With the advent of digital photography, and the wider sharing of scientific expertise through the Internet, even the most 'difficult' and inconspicuous moths are now the focus of unprecedented interest. Families that were once the domain of specialists, such as the tiny yet intricately patterned Gracillariidae or the fearsomely numerous Gelechiidae, have begun to filter into a public culture of 'Lepidopterology' as never before. Even in intensively studied regions such as Europe, new species of moths are still regularly turning up in more remote areas such as the mountainous interior of the Iberian Peninsula. Cities can also throw up surprises: in the summer of 2003, for example, a new species of moth was discovered on London's Hampstead Heath – although *Prays peregrina* is almost certainly a stowaway with food or horticultural imports, it has never been found outside the UK. It is now quite frequent in and around London but remains unknown in the rest of the world – its closest relative was described in a scientific journal from colonial Bombay in 1914.[61] Another recent addition to the European fauna is the Horse-chestnut Leaf Miner, *Cameraria ohridella*, first described in Macedonia in 1986 and now widespread across Europe; the reason for its rapid range extension is not fully understood, but we do know from nineteenth-century herbaria collections that the species was present all along in the Balkans, but had simply been overlooked.

This rise of popular interest comes at a time when the traditional sources of entomological knowledge, namely natural history museums located in the global North, face an unprecedented crisis in funding. Huge collections of specimens, some of which date back to the earliest scientific surveys, are held in Berlin, London, Munich, New York, Paris, Vienna and Washington, DC, among others. Yet there remain many thousands – probably millions – of unidentified insects in the labyrinthine corridors of these museums: there is simply not enough research money, nor time available, to sort through all the specimens. The pattern is increasingly one of limited systematic studies focused on quirks of curatorial interest or isolated doctoral projects, and as experienced taxonomists retire they leave behind increasing numbers of 'orphan taxa' for which there are no longer any experts available.[62]

The established model of the expert curator has been challenged by a new emphasis on hypothesis-driven molecular research, which is perceived to be more scientific than traditional taxonomic study. Recent advances in what has been termed 'DNA barcoding' may yet unsettle existing taxonomic knowledge of moths by displacing a reliance on morphological differences with the analysis of short genetic sequences that are easily obtained from any stage of an insect's life cycle. For its proponents, such as Daniel Janzen, the use of DNA barcoding is a critical tool in the face of the 'double crisis' facing biodiversity, stemming from the decline of taxonomy as a cutting-edge scientific field and huge gaps in current knowledge about nature.[63] The introduction of DNA barcoding techniques since the early 2000s has begun to reveal the presence of so-called 'cryptic species', which are morphologically indistinguishable from one another yet genetically distinct, suggesting that levels of biodiversity may be even higher than previously estimated. Scientists are able to use DNA barcoding to determine the precise 'genetic distance' between species, thereby solving many long-standing taxonomic riddles. A major project on European moths at Munich's Zoologische Staatssammlung (ZSM), for example, has also highlighted the cost-effectiveness of this approach in comparison with more labour-intensive forms of traditional taxonomy.[64]

For detractors, however, the advent of DNA barcoding disturbs the analytical emphasis of taxonomy on the organism as a whole. The object of research – a short sequence of DNA – is increasingly alienated from the original organism, whether a museum specimen or living creature.[65] For the anthropologist Stefan Helmreich, this means that we increasingly encounter 'biology unbound', where 'life is becoming unmoored from the boundaries of the organism into networks of connection'.[66] For now, however, it still seems unlikely that the molecular realm will be able to displace the continuing need for field-based research or the labour-intensive study of individual specimens.

2 Appellations

Natural history is nothing more than the nomination of the
visible.
Michel Foucault[1]

The English word 'moth' is of Germanic origin, and can be traced
to the Old English *moththe* or *moððe*, similar to the Northumbrian
mohðe, derived in turn from the Old Norse *motti*. Until the sixteenth
century, however, the word 'moth' was mainly used in relation to
the larvae of some species that devour clothes and fabrics. The Old
Testament's Book of Isaiah, for example, uses the clothes moth as
a warning – 'For the moth shall eat them up like a garment, and
the worm shall eat them like wool' – while in the New Testament's
Gospel of St Matthew, Jesus warns against worldly goods ('Lay
not up for yourselves treasures on earth where moth and rust doth
corrupt.')[2] The clothes moth also makes an appearance in Shakespeare's *Coriolanus*, where Penelope laments that 'all the yarn she
spun on Ulysses' absence did but fill Ithaca full of moths' (1.3). The
modern usage has diverged, however, since the English word
'moth' is now used for all moths, whereas the closely related
German word *Motte*, along with its Dutch and Scandinavian
counterparts, is restricted to species that eat clothes, grain and
other stored products.

One of the earliest words used for both moths and butterflies is the Greek word *psykhe* (*psychê*), first used by Aristotle,
which also refers to the human soul.[3] In its modern English usage,
however, via the Latin *psyche*, it has acquired a narrower meaning as 'spirit', and even more recently a scientific sense through

42

'psychology' and related terms.[4] There is, however, an earlier word, *phalaene* (similar to the modern Italian *falena*), that may be related to either the Latin word *phallus* derived from the Greek φαλλός (*phallós*), perhaps a reference to the shape of the insect's body rather than its wings, or to the Greek φως (*phos*), meaning light, implying either the pale colour of the wings or the attraction of moths to light.[5]

The Latin word *papilio* is often assumed to only mean butterflies, but Ovid uses the word to refer to moths in his *Metamorphoses*. He mentions 'worms that weave their white cocoons on the leaves of trees (a fact well known to country folk)', probably referring to silk moths as there are no butterflies that spin cocoons, and notes that they subsequently 'change into funereal butterflies' which may be an observation on the sombre markings of some moths or a recurring association with the human soul.[6] Pliny the Elder is also clearly referring to moths when he considered the *papilio* to be 'a cowardly and ignoble creature that flutters up to lamps when they are lit,

The evocatively named Merveille du Jour, *Dichonia aprilina*, emerges in the autumn and has similar colours and patterns to lichens that grow on trees.

and is destructive and inimical to bees'.[7] In this passage Pliny is likely to be describing the Wax Moth, *Galleria mellonella*, which has long been known to damage beehives.

The rich diversity of vernacular English names speaks to a significant place for moths in late seventeenth- and eighteenth-century cultures of nature: in the illustrated books of naturalists such as James Petiver and Moses Harris, many of the now familiar names can be found, if not in a slightly different form. In *The English Lepidoptera; Or, the Aurelians's Pocket Companion*, published in 1775, for example, Harris refers to the Cream-spot Tiger, *Arctia villica*, the Nettle-tap, *Anthophila fabriciana*, the Pale Tussock, *Calliteara pudibunda*, and many other names that are still in use.[8] Other eighteenth-century volumes such as Benjamin Wilkes's *English Moths and Butterflies, Representing their Changes into the Caterpillar, Chrysalis, and Fly States, and the Plants, Flowers, and Fruits, Whereon They Feed* (*c.* 1749) include several names that are now lost, but the species can easily be identified from the plates: Wilkes's 'Richmond Beauty' is the Lilac Beauty, *Apeira syringaria*, his 'Olive-Shades' is the Lime Hawk-moth, *Mimas tiliae* and his 'Unicorn' is the Convolvulus Hawk-moth, *Agrius convolvuli*.[9] Sometimes these names were simply coined by naturalists themselves, but in other cases they clearly already existed in language and folklore. The English entomologist, botanist and carcinologist (crustacean expert) Adrian Hardy Haworth (1767–1833) remarked in his multi-volume *Lepidoptera Britannica*, published between 1803 and 1828, that 'some of the English appellations . . . are highly fanciful, not to say absurd'.[10] Haworth recorded various words used for moth, including 'miller', a widely used name for any large moth, 'bustards' or 'owls' for larger moths in Westmoreland (possibly linked to the contemporary use of 'owlets' in North America) and 'soles', used in Lincolnshire and Yorkshire to refer to moths that fly into candles, no doubt related to the widespread belief that moths were human spirits.[11]

Many contemporary vernacular names, especially those drawn from the historical insights of natural history, refer to the larval foodplants of caterpillars: the Alder Kitten, *Furcula bicuspis*, the Barberry Carpet, *Pareulype berberata*, the Oak Beauty, *Biston strataria* and the Huckleberry Sphinx, *Paonias astylus*, to name but a few. Strange anomalies exist, however, such as the Horse Chestnut Moth, *Pachycnemia hippocastanaria*; whose vernacular and scientific names refer to a tree that has nothing to do with the moth's ecology or life history (the caterpillar feeds on heather).

Vernacular names have also been derived from patterns or colours: examples include the Peach Blossom, *Thyatira batis*, with wings adorned with markings like pale pink petals, and the Maiden's Blush, *Cyclophora punctaria*, that has small scarlet patches on each forewing. The Burnished Brass, *Diachrysia chrysitis* and *D. stenochrisis*, is among many moths that have shiny metallic markings, along with the Gold Spangle, *Autographa bractea*, known as *la feuille d'or* in French. The poetic cadence of vernacular names forms part of a cultural fascination with moths. Names such as the Merveille du Jour, *Dichonia aprilina*, or the Green-brindled Crescent, *Allophyes oxyacanthae*, evoke a sense of wonder that connects disparate fields such as folklore, place names and early scientific treatises.

The distinction between the English words 'moth' and 'butterfly' is often less apparent in other languages. In Spanish, for instance, the word *mariposa* is used to refer to both butterflies and moths, as is the French *papillon*, the German *Schmetterling* and the Swedish *fjäril*. It is, however, the association of moths with the night that stands out since the majority of species are nocturnal: hence we also have the French *papillons de nuit*, the German *Nachtfalter* and the Spanish *mariposa nocturna*. In Italian the situation is slightly more complicated since we have two words: *farfalla*, meaning butterfly, and *falena*, which can mean any Lepidoptera that fly by night or, more specifically, the moths of the family Geometridae

'le cui larve divorano i germogli degli alberi a primavera' (whose larvae devour buds in the spring).[12] However, *falena* also has meanings that refer more tangentially to moth-like characteristics: it can mean the thin layer of ash that remains on glowing coals or the darkened residues of burnt paper; a fickle, lively or vivacious young person; or more pejoratively *una donna leggera* (a female street-walker) or prostitute.[13] Like many other European languages there is an alternative Italian word, *tignola*, reserved for those species, and in particular their larvae, that eat clothes and other types of organic matter.

In East Asian languages we encounter a somewhat different set of cultural and etymological entanglements. In Korean, the word for moth 나방 (*nabang*) combines the meanings 'fly' or 'flutter' with that of 'lift up'. The Chinese word for moth 蛾 (*é*) uses various prefixes to denote different families. For example, 尺蛾 (*Chǐ'é*) combines the character for moth with a character meaning 'inch' and refers to the Geometridae 夜蛾 (*Yè'é*). The word 蚕蛾 (*cán'é*) refers to the silk moth where the prefix 蚕 means 'silkworm'. The symbol for silk 丝 (*si/sī*) is very frequent in Chinese: of the 5,000 most common characters used in Mandarin, 230 incorporate it, including the words for red, 红, and green, 绿, in recognition of the vibrant colours of silk fabrics.[14]

The Japanese *kanji* for moth is adapted from Chinese characters. It is derived from two *kanjis*: 虫 (*mushi*) meaning 'insect' and 我 (*ga*) meaning 'good shape'. Together they produce 蛾 meaning 'an insect with an orderly tactile sense'. In Japanese this *kanji* has a number of possible meanings: it can refer to a type of insect that flies at night or rests with its wings open or folding like a roof. A closely related *kanji*, 蛾眉 (*gabi*), means a 'beautiful eyebrow' which is 'long and slender and shaped like a moth's antenna' (the *kanji* for moth, 蛾, is very similar to 娥 (*ga*), which means beautiful). The related *kanji* for butterfly is also derived from 虫 (*mushi*),

The Maiden's Blush, *Cyclophora punctaria*, has a vernacular English name that pre-dates its Latin scientific name.

The Burnished Brass, *Diachrysia stenochrisis*, is named after the shining metallic pattern on its forewings that is produced by the interference effects of wing scales rather than pigments.

meaning 'insect', combined with 枼 (*you*), which is, in turn, an old form of the *kanji* for leaf 葉 (*ha*). Together, they produce 蝶 (*chou*) meaning 'an insect that flies with wings like leaves'.

The closest we have to an internationally understood set of names for moths is derived from Latin, the lingua franca of natural history since the European Renaissance. The key moment in the use of Latin for the scientific naming of moths and butterflies is the publication in 1758 of the tenth edition of the *Systema naturae* by the Swedish naturalist Carl Linnaeus.[15] This work marks the origins of the modern binomial (two-part) system of scientific nomenclature, in which an organism is identified by a first part denoting its genus (an intermediate taxonomic grouping between that of a family and a species) and then a second term defining its species (ordinarily defined as the largest group of organisms that can interbreed to produce fertile offspring). The Latin name is completed with details of the original describer and the year in which the first published description of the species appears. Hence we have, for example, the Heart Moth, *Dicycla oo* (Linnaeus, 1758), where the 'oo' simply refers to the distinctively shaped markings on the wings. In a further twist of convention the describer's name is placed in parentheses if the original genus has changed due to advances in taxonomic research: in the case of *Dicycla oo*, the original genus *Phalaena* suggested by Linnaeus (who only used three genera) was replaced in 1852 with *Dicycla* by the French entomologist Achille Guenée (1809–1880), and this name is now accepted as correct. The new system of names put forward by Linnaeus was quickly adopted by other scientists: the first purely entomological works to use it were the *Icones insectorum rariorum*, published from 1759 onwards by the Swedish entomologist Carl Alexander Clerck, and the 1761 publication *Insecta Musei Graecensis* by the Austrian entomologist Nikolaus Poda von Neuhaus.[16]

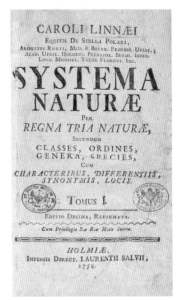

Every scientific name holds a small fragment of history. The insect collections in natural history museums are much more than a menagerie of dead specimens: they offer a window into the colonial antecedents of modern taxonomy. Consider the Ailanthus Silk Moth, originating from China and Korea, first placed within the framework of modern taxonomy with a description by the English silversmith and naturalist Dru Drury (1727–1803), who gave it the full scientific name of *Samia cynthia* (Drury, 1773). Since Drury travelled little, he probably only encountered this moth as a cultural artefact, yet his name remains memorialized instead of the non-Europeans to whom the moth was already known as a wild source of silk.

Nonetheless, the Linnaean system of nomenclature remains in place and is overseen by the International Commission on Zoological Nomenclature (ICZN), a body set up in 1895 to achieve

The title page from Carl Linnaeus, *Systema naturae* (1758).

The Swedish scientist Carl Linnaeus depicted by Alexander Roslin in 1775. Linnaeus was the founder of the binomial system of scientific nomenclature.

'stability and sense in the scientific naming of animals'.[17] In the nineteenth century, before the adjudicating role of the ICZN, bitter disputes erupted between rival lepidopterists over first claim to describe a new species. The ICZN was designed to arbitrate these disagreements and to avoid potential confusion caused by the proliferation of 'synonyms', where one organism can end up having several different names over time. The ICZN continues to perform this role today by ensuring that the 'law of priority' is upheld and the first accepted name takes precedence over any subsequent redescriptions by those covetous of leaving a taxonomic trace for posterity.

In his *Systema naturae* Linnaeus provides Latin names for 542 species of moths and butterflies, and though his system of classifying Lepidoptera has been completely overhauled, the individual species names remain in use. His nomenclature reveals much about the cultural sources of scientific authority in the eighteenth century and in particular the importance of classical mythology. For example, the Latin name for the Death's-head Hawk-moth is *Acherontia atropos*, the word *atropos,* chosen by Linnaeus, referring to one of the three Fates in Greek mythology. Linnaeus's original genus *Sphinx* was replaced in 1809, when the German entomologist Jakob Heinrich Laspeyres suggested *Acherontia*, a reference to the mythological River Acheron (according to the ancient Greeks, Acheron was the river where Charon, the ferryman of Hades, plied his trade, carrying the dead into the underworld). The other two species of Death's-head Hawk-moths, both found in Asia, are named after this theme: *Acherontia styx*, coined by the English entomologist and archaeologist John Obadiah Westwood in 1847, refers to another of the mythological rivers of the underworld, while *Acherontia lachesis*, first described by the Danish zoologist Johan Christian Fabricius in 1798, is named after the Greek Fate Lachesis. With this example and many others we can see how successive generations of entomologists have woven aspects of mythology and cultural history into the ostensible neutrality of scientific nomenclature.[18] The cultural association of this particular moth with death, however, can be traced much earlier than Linnaean taxonomy: it is probable that Pliny the Elder, in his *Natural History* (77 CE), is referring to this species with the name *Papilio feralis*, 'the butterfly that brings death'.[19]

Linnaeus and his followers cast their nets widely when it came to coining names. There are examples cribbed from earlier entomological literature, such as *cossus* and *vinula*, used by Thomas Moffet in his *Theatrum insectorum* (1634), and subsequently employed by Linnaeus for the Goat Moth, *Cossus cossus*, and the Puss Moth, *Cerura vinula*.[20] There are names derived from descriptive details, such as the Silver Y, *Autographa gamma*, which has metallic Y-shaped markings on its wings. There are also descriptors based on the resemblance to other organisms, such as *Bembecia ichneumoniformis* and *Synanthedon vespiformis*, which both refer to the resemblance of these moths to wasps, or that indicate a particular type of habitat preference, such as *Xanthorhoe montanata* (from 'mons' meaning mountain) or *Ostrinia palustralis* (from 'palus' meaning marsh). Other examples reflect the season of emergence or time of appearance, such as *Ennomos autumnaria* and *Ectropis crepuscularia* (from 'crepusculum' meaning twilight), or honour friends and colleagues, such as *Lyonetia clerkella* and *Conistra staudingeri*. We encounter many examples that flow from aesthetic appreciation, such as *Utetheisa pulchella* and *Epicallima formosella* from the Latin adjectives *pulcher* and *formosus* meaning beautiful. There are even names that are essentially head-scratchers, indicating a particular difficulty with classification, such as *Polymixis dubia* (from the Latin *dubium* meaning doubt), as well as names that stem from mere 'fancy'.[21] In general, however, most scientists have followed the Linnaean tradition of choosing names without any explanation: they simply remain puzzles to be solved by others.

The etymology of scientific names illuminates not only some of the more eccentric dimensions to science but provides insights into prevailing cultural attitudes towards distinctly non-scientific matters such as sex and marriage.[22] The genus *Catocala*, for instance, includes the spectacular 'red underwings', which flash their brightly coloured hindwings in defence against birds and other predators. The word *Catocala* is derived from the Greek κάτω (*kato*) meaning 'behind' and καλὸς (*kalos*) meaning 'beautiful'. The earliest of the described *Catocala* species are *Catocala pacta*, named by Linnaeus in 1758, from the Latin *pacta* meaning 'betrothed', and *Catocala nupta*, which Linnaeus first described in 1767 using the Latin word *nupta* meaning 'bride'. A welter of related names have followed: we have *Catocala promissa*, first described by the Austrian naturalists Michael Denis and Ignaz Schiffermüller in 1775, from *promissus* meaning 'promised or pledged in marriage'; *Catocala elocata*, named by the German entomologist Johann Christoph Esper in 1788, from *elocatus* denoting 'one hired out, a prostitute'; *Catocala nymphagoga*, also named by Esper in 1788, from *nymphagogos* or 'one who leads the bride from her home to the bridegroom's house'; and *Catocala electa*, chosen by Karl Friedrich Vieweg in 1790, from *electa* meaning 'fiancée'.[23] If we follow the naming of new *Catocala* species into the nineteenth century, the theme is continued with *Catocala dilecta*, classified by Jacob Hübner in 1803 and named after *dilecta*, the 'beloved'; *Catocala lupina*, named by Gottlieb A. W. Herrich-Schäffer, 1851, from *lupa* meaning 'she-wolf'; *Catocala adultera* described by Edouard Ménétriés in 1856, and so on. It is only through the evident exhaustion of this gendered trope that we begin to find *Catocala* species in Europe named after more

mundane associations or esteemed colleagues. The lack of any necessary connection between these gendered terms and the moths themselves is illustrated by North American names for the genus, most of which are connected with darkness, suffering and death: *Catocala insolabilis*, the 'inconsolable'; *Catocala dejecta*, the 'dejected'; *Catocala lacrymosa*, the 'tearful'; and *Catocala flebilis*, the 'doleful', to name but a few.[24] The gendering of scientific names, exemplified by the *Catocala* genus in Europe, illustrates the degree to which entomology, as a largely male scientific pursuit, projected its own conceptions of gender and social order onto its classificatory schema. It was still controversial, after all, in the late eighteenth century to even suggest that plants reproduced sexually.[25]

The Death's-head Hawk-moth was also known as the 'Bee Robber' because it steals honey from bee-hives. It gives off a specific scent that fools bees into thinking it is one of them. The death's head pattern may serve a protective function by resembling the face of a queen bee.

From these different sources of caprice and imagination, an intricate and often puzzling poetry of scientific names has evolved. The writings of the Russian novelist Vladimir Nabokov is full of allusions to names of butterflies and moths, often involving puns or references to earlier vernacular forms in order to play games with his readers. The title of his final novel, *Look at the Harlequins!* (1974), for example, may be a reference to the earlier vernacular name for the Magpie Moth, *Abraxas grossulariata*.[26] In some cases Nabokov simply invented scientific names for fun, such as the fictitious Geometrid Moth, *Austautia simonoides*, that appears in *The Gift* (1935–7).[27]

The strange cadence of Latin names also forms part of the inspiration for the English composer Sir Harrison Birtwistle's choral work *The Moth Requiem* (2012), a nineteen-minute piece scored for twelve female voices, three harps and an alto flute. At the centre of the work is a poem written by Robin Blaser in the early 1960s inspired by a strange sound in his house that he eventually traced to a moth trapped inside a piano that was repeatedly bumping into the strings in an effort to escape. The twelve singers incant the scientific names of twelve moths that are no longer found in Britain, such as *Scopula immorata*, last seen in East Sussex in 1961, *Depressaria discipunctella*, last recorded in Oxfordshire in 1924, and *Euclemensia woodiella*, the mysterious Manchester Moth, which we encounter in the next chapter. This requiem for lost moths, and their strangely evocative names, is connected for Birtwistle with childhood memories, the loss of loved ones and his own looming mortality.[28]

The names of moths, both vernacular and scientific, provide fascinating glimpses into diverse cultures of nature and the gradual

The Heart Moth, *Dicycla oo*. The Latin name 'oo' given by Linnaeus refers to the pattern on the wings.

The Red Underwing, *Catocala nupta*. In Europe the scientific names of the red underwings have focused on gender, sex and marriage while in North America the scientific names generally refer to distressed states of mind.

dominance of the Linnaean binomial system. The fact that many species from what is now known as the global South were first named and described by scientists from Europe, and more recently North America, reveals much about the colonial context for the emergence of modern taxonomy. The prevalence of gendered language similarly reveals the way that cultural attitudes are imbricated in the act of scientific naming. Scientific names, along with their contestation and regulation, form a complex component of the politics of nature: if Latin has served as an integral dimension to international scientific discourse since the Renaissance, it is interesting to reflect on whether new scientific developments such as DNA barcoding might yet engender novel approaches to the classification and naming of nature.

Maggie Taylor, *The Moth House*, 2012, photo collage.

3 Aurelians

Only in extinction is the collector comprehended.
Walter Benjamin[1]

Moths are present in some of the earliest writing on natural history. Aristotle, in his *Historia animalium* (350 BCE), provides a remarkably comprehensive account of the extent of zoological knowledge in his time. Several species of moths can be identified from his text including the Wax Moth, *Galleria melonella*, which is noted as a pest of beehives (he devotes a large part of his text to bees), at least one species of clothes moth, and what is likely to be the Magpie Moth, *Abraxas grossulariata*, a strikingly marked species whose caterpillars eat gooseberries, spindle, cherry and other trees.[2] Pliny the Elder, writing some four centuries later, devoted most of his life to the study of nature, including extensive observations on insects. For Pliny, insects revealed 'a craftsmanship on the part of nature that is more remarkable than in any other case'.[3] After the magisterial works of Aristotle and Pliny, however, the study of insects was neglected in Europe until the sixteenth century. The dominant source available in the Middle Ages was the *Physiologus*, a first-century work of unknown origin, which was for a time considered heretical, its pages dominated by symbolism rather than observation: the clothes moth, for example, represented temptations of the flesh while the bee epitomized virginity and wisdom. One of the only figures during this long period concerned with advancing knowledge of entomology was the German Dominican friar and Catholic bishop Albert von Bollstädt (*c.* 1193–1280), known as Albertus Magnus, who completed a zoological work *De animalibus* between 1255 and 1270. Magnus can best be placed in the vanguard of a pre-Renaissance reprise of interest in Aristotle's ideas (along with Arabic translations of these early works), which marked an attempt to demonstrate a degree of scientific independence from theological doctrine as well as to conserve earlier sources of knowledge.[4]

During the sixteenth century, however, we find a renewed interest in natural history as part of a wider rediscovery of the works of antiquity. A new cultural elite emerges in Renaissance Europe, emanating in particular from the Italian city-states, and using Latin as a common scientific language to foster the circulation of ideas.[5] Despite the re-emergence of interest in nature, however, insects remained a relatively neglected field in comparison with larger animals, and especially plants, until the late seventeenth century.[6] An exception is the Italian botanist Ulisse Aldrovandi (1522–1605), who was regarded by Linnaeus as the founder of modern natural history. Aldrovandi assembled a large collection of specimens, founded the Bologna botanical garden in 1568, and published one of the first comprehensive works devoted to entomology, *De animalibus insectis* (1602).[7]

The first major work on insects to appear in England is the post-humously published *Theatrum insectorum* (1634), by the English naturalist and physician Thomas Moffet (1553–1604).[8] Although Moffet completed the work in 1589, he could not find a publisher in his own lifetime. The book is actually derived from several earlier sources, including the unpublished works of the entomologist and physician Thomas Penny (1532–*c*. 1589), which in turn drew on materials by the naturalists Edward Wotton (1492–1555) and Conrad Gessner (1516–1565). The book includes many illustrations, among them pictures of moths that have not been recorded in Britain (perhaps reflecting the European origins of some of the source materials used by Moffet, or alternatively, a clue to lost fauna). When

Plate from Ulisse
Aldrovandi,
*De animalibus
insectis* (1602).

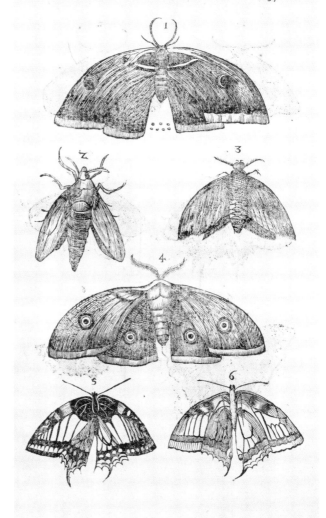

it was finally published, the work proved so popular that an English translation of the Latin quickly followed, allowing the book to reach an even wider audience.[9]

Further important contributions during the seventeenth century include those of the Italian pioneer of modern histology and microscopy Marcello Malpighi (1628–1694), who drew some of the first magnified depictions of insects, and discovered the respiratory organs of silkworms and other caterpillars in his *Dissertatio epistolica de Bombyce* (1663). The understanding of the life cycle of Lepidoptera was also advanced by the Italian physician Francesco Redi (1626–1698), who demonstrated conclusively that caterpillars and other insect larvae develop from eggs, and by the Dutch biologist Jan Swammerdam (1637–1680), who also revealed continuities between different life stages. Like Malpighi, Swammerdam drew extensively on dissection and microscopy to supplement the observation of living insects for his *Historia insectorum generalis* (1669).[10] He was particularly fascinated by insect metamorphosis, which provided a resonant symbol for his evangelical Protestantism.[11]

Further advances were made by the French scientist René-Antoine Ferchault de Réaumur (1683–1757), whose six-volume *Mémoires pour servir à l'histoire des insectes*, published between 1734 and 1742, is widely considered to be the first major work of modern entomology, and includes many species depicted at different stages of their life cycles.[12] As a mathematician who switched his attention to the search for patterns in nature, Réaumur was influential in bringing a more rigorous approach to natural history as a central element in the development of the empirical sciences.[13] In a similar vein to Réaumur, between 1752 and 1778 the Swedish entomologist Charles De Geer published his eight-volume *Mémoires pour servir à l'histoire des insectes*, which includes descriptions of many species of moths and other insects, but his

René-Antoine Ferchault de Réaumur (1683–1757). Réaumur made pioneering observations of moths and other insects.

Plate showing variations in moth antennae from René-Antoine Ferchault de Réaumur, *Mémoires pour servir à l'histoire des insectes* (1734–42).

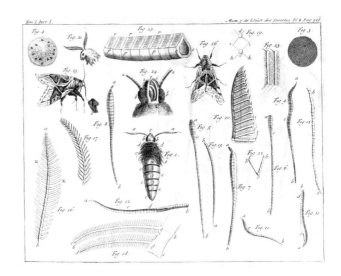

work proved of less long-term significance than that of his Swedish contemporary Carl Linnaeus.[14]

During the eighteenth century most works of natural history adopted various forms of 'natural theology', rooted in the belief that the study of nature allowed insights into divine wisdom. The English naturalist John Ray, for example, published *The Wisdom of God Manifested in the Works of Creation* (1691) in which he declared that 'if the number of creatures be so exceeding great, how great, nay, immense, must needs be the power and wisdom of him who formed them all!'[15] The influence of natural theology is also present in *The Aurelian* (1766) by the English naturalist and illustrator Moses Harris, where he recites Psalm 104: 24: 'O Lord, how manifold are thy Works! in Wisdom hast thou made them all: the Earth is full of thy Riches!'[16]

Harris relied on wealthy patrons who wished to own lavishly illustrated entomological books, capitalizing on the increasing

The Works of the Lord are Great, Sought out of all them that have Pleasure therein. Ps CXI.v.2.

Frontispiece from Moses Harris, *The Aurelian or Natural History of English Insects: Namely, Moths and Butterflies. Together with the plants on which they feed* (1766).

public appetite for natural history written in English rather than the traditional, scholarly Latin.[17] The elaborate and expensive plates for *The Aurelian* illustrate moths found in and around London, and were dedicated to various international sponsors and benefactors, including Linnaeus and the merchant and naturalist Dru Drury, suggesting a new exchange of knowledge across national borders within Europe. The gradual adoption of a standardized taxonomic

N. Jones ad Vivum Sculp

To my Ingenous Friend and Benefactor Mr Dru Drury
This Plate is most Humbly Dedicated by his Obliged Servant Moses Harris

system at this time can be seen in the fact that Harris did not use Linnaean nomenclature in the first edition of *The Aurelian* but adopted the binomial system for his later work nine years later, *The Aurelian's Pocket Companion* (1775).[18]

Early modern natural history books form part of the history of publishing: changes in production technologies from crude woodcut reliefs to copper intaglio and finally to lithography led to an improvement in the quality and availability of printed works. These illustrated books – for which Lepidoptera, with their vibrant colours and fascinating markings, provided ideal subject-matter – offered opportunities to showcase new production techniques while creating highly prized cultural artefacts. With their vivid hand-coloured plates, natural history books became part of the 'symbolic capital' of their age and were eagerly sought after. New approaches to the setting and presentation of entomological specimens, 'adding artificial to natural elegance', also became part of the panoply of techniques that transformed the living insect into an exquisite and collectable object.[19]

Amateur enthusiasts for butterflies and moths in seventeenth-century England described themselves as 'aurelians' – a word derived from the golden hue that the chrysalis of some butterflies acquires shortly before the adult insect emerges. In the 1690s around half a dozen entomologists formed the original yet short-lived Aurelian Society, which is believed to be one of the earliest zoological societies founded in Europe, and whose collection was consulted by leading scientists of the day such as John Ray. The sharing of specimens was a distinctive feature of early entomology and formed part of an emerging culture of curiosity towards nature: a condition of joining the Aurelian Society was that members had to donate specimens of any species not yet held in its collection.[20] The consolidation of disparate private endeavours formed part of a nascent public scientific culture that eventually contributed to

Plate showing Death's-head Hawk-moth from Moses Harris, *The Aurelian or Natural History of English Insects: Namely, Moths and Butterflies. Together with the plants on which they feed* (1766).

the emergence of natural history museums.[21] A second Aurelian Society, set up in London around 1738, also lasted only a few years, and opened up its collection to the public. Unfortunately, however, the society lost its entire collection to a fire in 1748.

If the development of a 'discerning eye' for nature characterized the growth of both scientific societies and a metropolitan market for illustrated works of natural history, it was also reflected in rather more exploitative relationships between collection and commerce. The earliest surviving insect collection from the seventeenth century originally belonged to the English apothecary and naturalist James Petiver (*c.* 1663–1718), and is now held in London's Natural History Museum. Petiver managed to assemble a vast and highly eclectic collection of insects, comprising specimens from the East Indies, the Caribbean and China, as well as 'moths from the English countryside', despite the fact that he travelled very little outside of London; this was thanks to the paid assistance of travellers and mariners, who included suitable hunting grounds for 'exotic' insects in their itineraries. Petiver was not simply a collector of insects but a 'collector of collectors', building a global network of contacts for the purchase and exchange of insects.[22]

In the eighteenth century, this often meant relying on ships involved in the slave trade to acquire specimens. 'Petiver's natural historical collections,' writes the historian Kathleen Murphy, 'reveal the entangled histories of the trade in human cargo and the exchange of natural curiosities in the late seventeenth- and early eighteenth-century British Atlantic.' Murphy recounts how Petiver asked a slave ship captain headed for Jamaica to 'lend my flycatchers to some of your blacks while your on the Island' and 'to take & kill whatever butterflies & Moths they meet'. Not only did Petiver request that the ship bring back interesting specimens from the Caribbean, but he clearly hoped that the free labour of slaves on board might be exploited to further his entomological endeavours.

Plate showing the Elephant Hawk-moth and other insects from Moses Harris, *The Aurelian or Natural History of English Insects: Namely, Moths and Butterflies. Together with the plants on which they feed* (1766).

For Murphy, a 'collecting gaze' extended from natural history, and the selection of zoological specimens, to the slave traders' differentiation between the value of one slave and another in their human cargoes.[23]

The connections between slavery and taxonomy also touched the work of Linnaeus, whose *Systema naturae* refers to illustrations from Petiver's *Gazophylacii naturæ & artis: decas tertia* (1704), including a moth that a ship's surgeon had collected on the coast of West Africa. Surgeons were present to benefit the slave traders by reducing the high mortality rates caused by atrocious conditions on ships, thereby boosting profits.[24] However, they also brought a broad-based scientific

68

approach to travel that helped to develop zoological, cartographical and geographical forms of knowledge. Although leading figures in the history of science such as Alexander von Humboldt (1769–1859) personally condemned slavery, the wider context of much scientific work was nevertheless reliant on its trade routes. Humboldt's own expeditions to Latin America between 1799 and 1804, and the early origins of isometric mapping and modern ecology, cannot be considered separately from the wider context of expanding European influence and nascent forms of global capitalism.

By the eighteenth century natural history had become the focal point for scientific research with collections of specimens serving as the equivalent of modern-day laboratories. Taxonomic advances were driven by new technologies of observation such as the microscope, a late sixteenth-century innovation, assiduously used for the study of insects, and particularly to sort and classify growing numbers of specimens. From the outset, however, there were tensions over how to interpret this vast amount of material. Earlier methods of study, such as that pioneered by Aldrovandi, were considered increasingly unsuitable for the needs of a more rigorous natural science.[25] While some scientists restricted themselves to largely enumerative or descriptive tasks, others such as Réaumur and Humboldt tried to discern patterns and relationships in nature.[26]

In a curious precursor to the digital age, the production of illustrated books proved more important than the circulation of specimens (which were frequently lost or damaged). Among the most famous entomological artists of this period is the Frankfurt-born naturalist and illustrator Maria Sibylla Merian (1647–1717), a contemporary of Petiver, who began her work with studies of silkworms and caterpillars that she found in her garden. Her intricate and highly stylized representations of insects, including details of different life stages, are among the most important examples of scientific illustration from this period, and emphasized relations between organisms rather than the morphological classification of individual specimens. Over time Merian became increasingly fascinated by 'exotic' specimens she had seen while living in Holland, and in 1699 she and her daughter emigrated to Suriname in order to study living insects more closely. Her attitude towards the Dutch colony was somewhat ambiguous since she clearly benefited indirectly from the sugar plantations while at the same time condemning the more egregious forms of misery and violence that she encountered.[27] She employed not only indigenous inhabitants to assist with her work but slaves, whom she referred to as 'myne . . . Indiaan and . . . Slaven'.[28] The frontispiece to her book *Metamorphosis insectorum Surinamenisum* (1719), engraved by Frederik Ottens, rather incongruously depicts white cherubs assisting Merian with her illustrations, although some of the real entomological labour can be seen in the background, including figures with butterfly nets.[29]

The book proved both popular and influential, especially for later figures such as Pieter Cramer (1721–1776), the Dutch merchant and entomologist, who specialized in tropical butterflies and moths. Both Merian and Linnaeus are honoured in the frontispiece to his vast work *De uitlandscke kapellen voorkomende in drie waereld-deelen Asia, Africa en America* (Exotic Lepidoptera from Three Regions of the World, Asia, Africa and America), published in parts between 1775 and 1782, which makes full use of Linnaean systematics to name hundreds of new species. Like Petiver, Cramer never collected in the field but relied on his trading connections to obtain specimens. After his death in 1776, his colleague Caspar Stoll, a former clerk turned entomologist, helped to complete the project, which is so comprehensive that it is still a point of reference today.[30]

After the publication of Linnaeus's *Systema naturae*, the study of moths advanced rapidly in Europe through a series of comprehensive regional studies. The Tyrolean naturalist Giovanni Antonio Scopoli adopted the 'Methodo Linnaeana' for his *Entomologia*

Arbre de Gomme gutte (Gummi Guttae Tree with White Witch, Cocoon, and Caterpillar of Hawk Moth and Drops of Resin) from Maria Sibylla Merian, *Metamorphosis insectorum Surinamenisum* (1719).

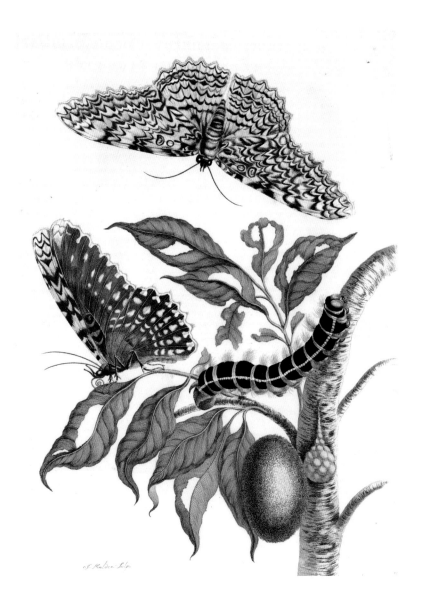

P. Sluyter sculp.

Michael Denis and Ignaz Schiffermüller, *Ankündung eines systematischen Werkes von den Schmetterlingen der Wienergegend* (1775). Denis, along with Moses Harris, was one of the earliest users of a 'colour wheel' to explore the diversity of colours in nature.

Carniolica (1763), which explores an area of the Austro-Hungarian Empire that now lies in western Slovenia.[31] Other important regional surveys include Otto Friedrich Müller's study of Copenhagen published in 1764, Johann Hufnagel's survey of Berlin and its environs published in 1766 and 1767 and, most extensive of all, Michael Denis and Ignaz Schiffermüller's study of the Vienna region published in 1775, which

Red Wine Grapes and Vine with Lepidoptera Metamorphosis from Merian's *Metamorphosis insectorum Surinamenisum.*

is arguably the most comprehensive and influential study of European Lepidoptera to be completed in the eighteenth century.[32]

Perhaps unsurprisingly, the nomenclature and taxonomy of Lepidoptera also developed rapidly. The Danish zoologist Johan Christian Fabricius (1745–1808), a pupil of Linnaeus, emerged as a leading systematist for the modernization and standardization of scientific knowledge, while his contemporary Jacob Hübner (1761–1826) made significant advances in entomological illustration, and also developed a modern taxonomic understanding of the concept of the genus. Ambitious and increasingly specialist works appeared, such as those by Franz von Paula Schrank (1747–1835), who completed a multi-volume study of Bavaria in 1803, and Ferdinand Ochsenheimer (1767–1822), who initiated a ten-volume study of Europe completed by his colleague Georg Friedrich Treitschke in 1834.[33] The taxonomic advances represented by this research were by no means universally accepted, however, as evidenced by the English entomologist William Kirby (1759–1850), who rejected the systematics of Fabricius, and his 'eagerness to innovate', in a politically charged scientific dispute that

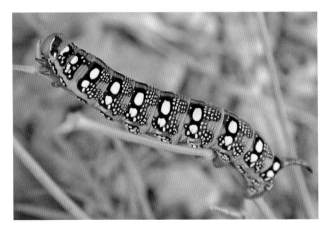

The caterpillar of the Spurge Hawk-moth, *Hyles euphorbiae*, the metamorphosis of which was a source of fascination for Goethe.

A page from the 19th-century field notebooks of the German lepidopterist Philipp Christoph Zeller (1824), who significantly advanced knowledge of the smaller Lepidoptera.

prefigured later struggles between natural theology and evolutionary theory.[34]

In the nineteenth century a new generation of Lepidopterists advanced knowledge in various ways. There were those who focused on particular groups or families, for example the work of the German entomologist Philipp Christoph Zeller on microlepidoptera. Others extended studies into little-known regions, exemplified by the German entomologist Otto Staudinger, who collected extensively in the Anatolian and Iberian peninsulas. Finally, in an elaboration of earlier connections established in the eighteenth century, expeditionary surveys or colonial posts were used as a base from which to conduct research, as illustrated by Enrico Festa in Ecuador, Henry Walter Bates in the Amazon basin (after whom Batesian mimicry, discussed in Chapter Seven, is named) and Arthur Gardiner Butler in New Zealand.

Other developments included the comparative analysis of the reproductive organs of Lepidoptera: for the first time, minute yet reliable differences between the genitalia of many hundreds of similar species were noted, which serve to prevent hybridization through intricate 'lock and key' type structures that only allow the same species to successfully mate. The most detailed and influential study of moths from nineteenth-century Europe is probably the six-volume series of the German entomologist Gottlieb A. W. Herrich-Schäffer, published between 1843 and 1856, which extended taxonomic studies to subtle differences in wing venation and other morphological features.[35] Meanwhile, in North America the second half of the nineteenth century saw a dramatic growth in entomology marked by increasing numbers of scientists, specialist journals and scientific articles. A distinctive emphasis on pest species marked the close relationship between government investment in entomology and the needs of capitalist agriculture, including the cotton plantations of the South (with their particular susceptibility to

Frontispiece by Frederik Ottens from Maria Sibylla Merian, *Metamorphosis insectorum Surinamenisum* (1719).

insect pests). The 'field orientation' of American entomology and its interest in population dynamics marked a significant precursor to the emergence of modern ecology and also facilitated an early acceptance of Darwinian theory among the scientific community. However, on both sides of the Atlantic, the increasing professionalization of entomology towards the later nineteenth century did little to redress the marginalization of women in the study of insects.[36]

During the nineteenth century increasing tensions emerged in the field of entomological taxonomy. The desire to be the 'first describer' of a species could provoke bitter disagreements as a cherished 'new species' became relegated to the status of a mere 'synonym' for a previously described taxon. Arguments over names became the focus of intense disputation between rivals: the prominent American lepidopterists Augustus R. Grote and Herman Strecker, for example, repeatedly tore into each other over the naming of new species, and resorted to ridiculing each other's scientific work. Grote, writing in 1881, chastised Strecker for his proliferation of names for previously described species:

> He has made proportionately more and more unexcusable synonyms than any other writer, and his slovenly descriptions and confessed unacquaintance with structure place him on a level with the worst amateur who has 'coined' a 'species'.[37]

Grote was no doubt piqued, however, by Strecker's review of his major work on North American moths that had been published just a few years earlier. 'The whole thing is scarcely worth the time devoted to this review,' Strecker had written:

> but as the advertisement would lead us to expect quite a different production, than that really furnished, we have given

The Manchester Moth or Manchester Tinea, *Euclemensia woodiella*, first described and illustrated by John Curtis in his *British Entomology* (1830). The moth has not been seen since 1829.

this cursory warning because the price demanded is entirely too big to pay for trunk paper.[38]

This high-profile episode may have served as the inspiration for a similar tale of bitter rivalry in H. G. Wells's short story 'The Moth', first published in 1895, which relays the 'Hapley–Pawkins feud' or 'the *odium theologicum* in a new form', played out in the pages of a respected entomological journal:

> It began years ago with a revision of Microlepidoptera (whatever these may be) by Pawkins in which he extinguished a new species created by Hapley . . . It was a long struggle, vicious from the beginning and growing at last to pitiless antagonism.[39]

As the war of words escalates, Hapley makes a final reply to Pawkins that 'left no loophole; it was murderous in argument, and utterly contemptuous in tone'. Pawkins dies without ever responding, only to be reincarnated as a rare and previously unknown moth. One evening, working in his study, Hapley feels the strange moth 'blunder into his face', and realizes immediately that it is of immense scientific interest. Unfortunately, however, the moth thwarts every attempt at capture, gradually driving him to a state of madness. Hapley ends the story tied to his bed and facing 'the remainder of his days in a padded room'.[40]

Another bizarre episode from the nineteenth-century world of moths concerns the now extinct *Euclemensia woodiella*, better known as the Manchester Moth or the Manchester Tinea. It was first discovered in the 1820s by the insect collector Robert Cribb as it flew around a rotting alder tree on Kersal Moor, near to what is now the Manchester racecourse. Cribb passed on specimens to the prominent nineteenth-century entomologist John Curtis (1791–1862), who published a scientific article in 1830 announcing the species as new to science. Unfortunately, both the article and the scientific name wrongly honoured Cribb's colleague, Mr R. Wood, with the discovery. To make matters worse Cribb suffered the further indignity of being accused of passing off 'foreign' specimens as British (a not-infrequent practice by unscrupulous dealers at the time). Cribb is reputed to have given up entomology and left his insect collection with his land-lady as debt security, but after he fell into arrears the collection was duly disposed of. Only three specimens of *Euclemensia woodiella* still exist – they are held by the Manchester Museum, London's Natural History Museum and Melbourne's Victoria Museum – and the moth has never been seen again.[41]

The accusations of fraud against the hapless Cribb are interesting because they illuminate the degree of suspicion that surrounded the burgeoning trade in rare insects that had developed since the eighteenth century. A relatively common species from continental Europe that could be passed off as a bona fide British specimen might fetch a hugely inflated price. A typical ruse by the so-called 'Kentish buccaneers' was to secretly import live specimens from Europe, and

The Clifden Nonpareil, *Catocala fraxini*, has been a source of apprehension and desire for British collectors since it was first encountered in the 18th century; it is found throughout much of Europe, and as far east as Japan.

then release them at selected sites ready for their re-capture as 'rare migrants', and subsequent sale to avid British collectors.[42] As early as 1829, for example, the English entomologist James Francis Stephens (1792–1852), after whom Stephens's Gem, *Megalographa biloba*, is named, noted that interest in specimens of rare British moths such as the wonderfully named Pease Blossom, *Periphanes delphinii*, was lessened 'by the execrable practice of introducing Continental insects into collections', in other words by 'cheating'.[43]

In Britain perhaps the most longed-for moth has been the Clifden Nonpareil, *Catocala fraxini*, the most spectacular of the European underwings, with blue rather than red hindwings. The moth, whose English vernacular name is derived from Cliefden (now Cliveden) in Buckinghamshire, where it was first encountered in the early eighteenth century, appears in the autumn and has occasionally been encountered at 'sugar' (a fermented concoction of molasses, beer and rum used to attract moths). The hope and anguish of finding this great rarity is captured by the English lepidopterist P.B.M. Allan:

> I am sure I shall find *C. fraxini* at my sugar one night, and then I shall be so scared that I shall bungle him hopelessly, and he will fly away over the tops of the trees, and I shall return home and sell my collection, and take to my bed and die.[44]

The excitement and tragicomedy of pursuing rare or elusive insects is ever present in the writing of Vladimir Nabokov, who was an avid collector since childhood. His early enthusiasm was inspired, in part, by his desire to find a species new to science and to see his name on a distinctive red label next to his original specimen (or 'holotype') in a museum collection. Nabokov describes how as a schoolboy in Russia he had yearned for the discovery of an unknown species of 'pug', a distinctive group of tiny Geometrid moths, which he describes as 'delicate little creatures that cling in the daytime to speckled surfaces, with which their flat wings and turned-up abdomens blend'.[45] Some 30 years later, writing his novel *Bend Sinister* in the u.s., Nabokov finally succeeded in finding his new pug on that 'blessed black night in the Wasatch Range' in August 1943. While staying at a guest lodge in Alta, twenty miles southeast of Salt Lake City, he caught a small pug resting on the plate glass window of the lounge and sent it to the eminent Canadian entomologist James McDunnough for identification. McDunnough confirmed that the moth was new to science and named it in his honour, *Eupithecia nabokovi*. 'I take great pleasure in dedicating this species to my friend, V. Nabokov,' wrote McDunnough, 'from whom I have received much interesting material in this genus for study.'[46] Nabokov's original Utah specimen still remains in Harvard University's Museum of Comparative Zoology next to its coveted red label. So intense were Nabokov's lepidopterological obsessions that they contributed to his death: he sustained serious injuries in a fall, from which he never fully recovered, while chasing butterflies on a Swiss mountainside, his net left hanging from a tree like 'Ovid's lyre'.[47]

The classic insect collection from the nineteenth century onwards consisted of several wooden cabinets, smelling strongly of naphthalene to ward off pests such as the museum beetle, *Anthrenus museorum*, which is capable of reducing an entire collection to dust (damage to specimens by 'animalculae' was noted as early as the eighteenth century by Moses Harris who used tobacco smoke to try and ward them off).[48] For some collectors, taxonomic advances that altered existing names or phylogenetic relationships not only provoked consternation but inconvenience, since the labels or physical arrangement of specimens in cabinets would have to be altered (including the blank spaces waiting to be filled). Although collections were often bequeathed to museums, the practice of assembling dead specimens has been increasingly viewed as anachronistic, eccentric or even inimical to nature – especially from the middle decades of the twentieth century onwards – with changing attitudes towards nature conservation. In reality, however, there are very few instances of even local extinctions being caused by collecting alone, although the ethical aspects of non-scientific collecting have become more questionable with increasing emphasis on other means of study such as photography.

Until the middle decades of the twentieth century, the creation of an insect collection was a common pastime, not so different from other forms of collecting such as books, coins or stamps. The German cultural critic Walter Benjamin, for example, created a small childhood collection of insects, caught mostly in his turn-of-the-century Berlin garden, for which the excitement of each addition was a formative memory:

> When in this way a vanessa or sphinx moth (which I should have been able to overcome easily) made a fool of me through its hesitations, vacillations, and delays, I would gladly have been dissolved into light and air, merely in order to approach my prey unnoticed and be able to subdue it.[49]

For Benjamin, every object holds its own memories, whether a moth caught in his garden or a rare volume spotted by chance in the unsorted corner of a secondhand bookshop. Collecting involves the liberation of the object of desire through its acquisition: by plucking an object from obscurity, or by finding something that no one else has noticed, the collector has the power to imbue meaning into the most esoteric of things.[50] The pursuit of a collection serves as a kind of 'renewal of existence', and is linked for Benjamin with the imaginative forays and inventories of children who amass their small collections of interesting objects such as leaves, stones and dead insects.

Yet collecting, it seems, has always been a somewhat male pursuit, notwithstanding notable exceptions such as Maria Sibylla

Merian, Annette Braun and Miriam Rothschild, or even the novelist Virginia Woolf, but the origins of this imbalance lie ultimately in society. The earlier predominance of men in natural history holds parallels with other cultural pursuits that require money, time and opportunities for independent travel, let alone acceptance within the rarefied realm of scientific societies or other kinds of social clubs. The desire to both know and control, and its intellectual lineage to the nascent field of taxonomy, has also been a focus of literature, where the insect collector has often been a somewhat suspect figure: secretive, obsessive or even dangerous, as in Arthur Conan Doyle's *Hound of the Baskervilles* (1902) or John Fowles's *The Collector* (1963).

Moths and other insects form one of the 'theaters of nature' that underpinned the growth of natural history as a critical part of the 'scientific revolution'.[51] As this chapter has shown, the history of entomology is also a history of collecting and colonialism, of publication and the public sphere, of profit and professionalism. Art, science and publishing were closely entwined through the development of natural history, whether in the vibrant tableaux of Harris and Merian, or through the gradual standardization of the colour identification plate with its serried ranks of taxonomically related species. As the earlier encyclopaedic endeavours, which reached their acme in the nineteenth century, were gradually displaced by recognition of the need to develop more focused and systematic fields of study, a more utilitarian perspective towards entomology began to take hold, as its contribution to agriculture, education, science and other fields was recognized. Yet the role of the individual collector or amateur enthusiast remains significant even today, and may become still more vital in the future, as new advances in cartography, photography and other fields, along with the communicative power of the Internet, mark the rise of the digital aurelian.

4 Drawn to the Flame

La farfalla, a lu lumi attornu vola (The moth always flies
around the light)
Sicilian proverb[1]

Thus hath the candle sing'd the moth.
O, these deliberate fools!
William Shakespeare, *The Merchant of Venice* (II.9)

The attraction of moths to light has probably received more attention than any other behavioural trait. Indeed it is often fatal: even
if moths are not burned by the candle flame or hot bulb, they are
often unable to draw themselves away. If they fly into buildings
they may become trapped, and if they are lured towards external
lights, they may settle nearby in exposed positions, vulnerable to
an array of predators such as bats, centipedes or lizards lurking
in the darkness. The cultural association of moths with light seems
to be very widespread: from the etymological traces in Greek
antiquity to 'the particular one which is fire crazy' in Navaho
mythology, the fateful behaviour of moths before fire or light can
be traced in almost every language and culture, from the earliest
use of fire to the latest forms of artificial light.[2]

The lure of light has often been portrayed as a metaphor for
doomed attraction in which the impassioned lover will surely die.
The Gulistan (The Rose Garden), written by the Persian poet Sheikh
Muslih-uddin Sa'di Shirazi (Sa'di of Shiraz) in 1259, includes the
theme of a lovestruck moth that is drawn to a flame like a flower:
'A devoted lover holds not back his hand from the object of his
affections though arrows and stones may rain upon his head.'[3]
Even where the object and outcome of desire are less clear, the
metaphor has remained a powerful one. In a painting by Balthus
entitled *The Moth* (1959–60), the artist uses a mosaic-like effect

Louis Busman,
Moth and Candle,
c. 1989.

to portray a naked woman juxtaposed with a moth flying around a candle. There are at least five elements of attraction depicted: candle, moth, woman, artist and audience. Described as having 'the texture of a rough stuccoed wall', Balthus's painting remains ambiguous: is the woman protecting the moth from the flame or actually luring it towards danger?[4]

The theme of the moth in love with the flame, burning up through its own mysterious passion, is also captured by Johann Wolfgang von Goethe in his poem *Selige Sehnsucht* (Ecstatic Longing), written in 1814. Goethe's moth is enthralled by the power of the light; longing to reach it, the moth refuses to heed the risks involved in approaching the flame, 'Till, poor moth, at last you perish/ In the flame, in love with light.'[5]

In 'Ecstatic Longing' Goethe brings together the themes of self-destruction and self-transformation. The parallel he draws between moth and lover consumed by their own passion as the 'soul's ecstatic absorption into God' draws on various influences, including Neoplatonic transcendentalism, Christian symbolism and Sufic mysticism.[6]

A sense of dignity in death for the burned moth is present in the work of the Lebanese-American painter and writer Kahlil Gibran (1883–1931), where the emphasis is on spiritual redemption rather than desire. In Gibran's novel *Al-Ajniha al-Mutakassira* (Broken Wings, 1912) he writes:

For the soul to experience torment because of its persever-ance in the face of trials and difficulties is more noble than for it to retreat to a place of safety and calm. The moth that continues to flutter about the lamp until it burns up is more exalted than the mole that lives in comfort and security in its dark tunnel.[7]

Yet in other cases, the attraction of moths to light is seen not so much as a mark of courage but as an opportunity to question foolish conformity. James Thurber's laconic tale 'The Moth and the Star', from his *Fables for our Time* (1940), describes a moth who ignores the advice of other moths to fly around a 'bridge lamp', and tries in vain to reach a star instead: although he never succeeds, he does survive into old age whereas his family are all 'burned to death when they were quite young'.[8] Thurber's moral? 'Who flies afar from the sphere of our sorrow is here today and here tomorrow.'

Although the relationship of moth to candle usually depicts a light source luring the hapless male lover, there are differently gendered configurations of the theme. In Cyprian Ekwensi's novel *People of the City* (1954), set in Lagos, the author describes 'girls who hovered around the glitter like moths', a symbol of the attractiveness of urban wealth held by men amid the burgeoning nightlife culture of pre-independence Nigeria.[9] In this sense the allure of light is used to depict Lagos as a 'fast city' on the cusp of a brief post-colonial efflorescence that preceded the Biafran civil war, petroleum-fuelled economic instability and the rise of military rule.

The disconcerting presence of moths and other nocturnal insects at light is vividly evoked by Jean Rhys in her novel *Wide Sargasso Sea* (1966), set in Jamaica and Dominica in the 1830s, in which she uses the swarming of insects around candles to instil an atmosphere of fecundity and unease. In one sequence she describes a candlelit meal with windows opened onto the humid night:

We drank champagne. A great many moths and beetles found their way into the room, flew into the candles and fell dead on the tablecloth. Amélie swept them up with a crumb brush. Uselessly. More moths and beetles came.[10]

As they step onto the veranda, they become suddenly aware of the night around them, from heavily fragrant flowers to singing insects:

> The long veranda was furnished with canvas chairs, two hammocks, and a wooden table on which stood a tripod telescope. Amélie brought out candles with glass shades but the night swallowed up the feeble light. There was a very strong scent of flowers – the flowers by the river that open at night she told me – and the noise, subdued in the inner room, was deafening. 'Crac-cracs,' she explained, 'they make a sound like their name, and crickets and frogs.'[11]

And then a huge moth entered the room:

> A large moth, so large I thought it was a bird, blundered into one of the candles, put it out and fell to the floor . . . I took the beautiful creature up in my handkerchief and put it on the railing. For a moment it was still and by the dim candlelight I could see the soft beautiful colours, the intricate pattern on the wings. I shook the handkerchief gently and it flew away.[12]

In these and other passages Rhys evokes a sense of nature as disconcerting and overwhelming: the chimera of an idyllic colonial life, and its indolence, is juxtaposed with more powerful forces extending to the sensual power of nature and impending political revolt.

The attraction of light for moths has also served as a form of political and philosophical allegory. Karl Marx, for example, in his notebooks on Epicurean philosophy, explores the tension between subjective consciousness and the material world, and describes how 'when the universal sun has gone down, the moth seeks the lamplight of the private individual'.[13] Here Marx uses the metaphor of the nocturnal moth entering an illuminated domestic interior to illustrate the regression from the universalism of Aristotelian philosophy to the inner world of post-Aristotelian philosophers such as Epicurus and Zeno.[14] Marx's metaphor has also been used for the collapse of state socialism in Eastern Europe and the frenzied divestment of state assets along with the rise of new and more intense forms of privatism.[15]

One of the most popular works of the Japanese artist Gyoshū Hayami, entitled *Dance of Flames* (1925), shows a swirl of moths around a column of fire. The inspiration for the painting came from Hayami's three-month sojourn in the mountain resort Karizawa, where he observed the strange dance-like movements of moths attracted to bonfires at night. Although the painting is considered a symbolist work of the Taishō period (1912–26), it combines elements of Buddhist imagery with direct observations of nature, including Hayami's attempt at an accurate depiction of the contrast between the brightness of the fire encircled by intense darkness.[16]

The attraction of moths to light has also been explored in surrealist art. Max Ernst, for example, in his collage entitled *et les papillons se mettent à chanter* (1929) shows moths and other insects flying around a gas lamp at night, while in the background skeletons begin to stir in their tombs. The streetlight, as a symbol par excellence of metropolitan modernity, is thus transformed into the focus of a disquieting and macabre scene. This work forms part of his pictorial compendium for the collage novel *La Femme 100 têtes* (1929), which also includes other uncanny infestations such as pigeons and grasshoppers.

Nineteenth-century entomologists made use of the attraction of moths and other insects to light, and taking a 'lantern into

Jean Rhys, *Wide Sargasso Sea* (1966), with cover design by Faith Jaques.

the woods' was part of the moth hunter's world long before sophisticated light traps were introduced in the 1950s. Farmers have also used fire to kill moths that threaten their crops: American cotton farmers, for example, used to light fires at night to kill 'bollworms' before pesticides were widely available (the name 'bollworm' actually refers to several moths, including *Helicoverpa armigera* in Europe and *Helicoverpa zea* and *Pectinophora gossypiella* in the usa).[17]

Yet while the attraction of moths to light is well known, the reason for this behaviour remains something of an enigma. Moths are not attracted to light in the sense that they might actively seek nectar or sugar, but are effectively compelled towards light by their neural networks. They become mesmerized under the glare and are often unable to fly away. Experiments during the twentieth century showed that it is not only the light intensity but the spectrum that is significant, with the ultraviolet range having the greatest behavioural effects. The classic Robinson Moth Trap, with its powerful mercury vapour bulb, emerged during the early 1950s from this stage of light experimentation and remains one of the most effective and widely used types of entomological field equipment to this day.

The precise mechanisms by which moths are attracted to light have been subject to much speculation. At least four

The Norwegian photographer Kjell B. Sandved in Venezuela in the late 1960s.

Gyoshū Hayami,
Dance of Flames,
1925, painting
on silk.

Max Ernst,
*et les papillons
se mettent à
chanter* (And
the Butterflies
Begin to Sing),
1929, illustration.

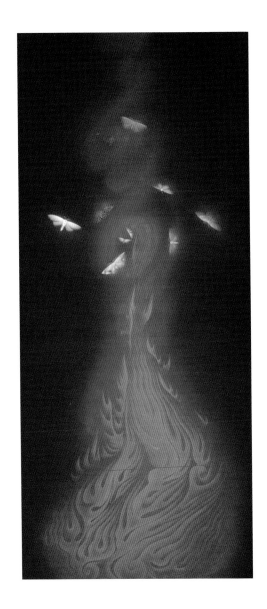

different explanations have been put forward. Firstly, the 'light compass' or 'moon theory' suggests that moths evolved under conditions when the only principal sources of light at night would have been the moon or stars. Their navigation systems make use of 'transverse orientation' whereby they travel at a constant angle in relation to distant sources of light. When confronted with a source of illumination in closer proximity, such as a candle or a streetlight, this mechanism is affected and they begin to spiral ever nearer. There is certainly evidence that on nights with a full moon, artificial light sources (including moth traps) are less attractive to moths, but this may simply be due to cooler temperatures under a clear sky.[18] Doubts about the 'moon theory' have been raised by the American entomologist Jerry Powell, since only migratory moths are likely to be reliant on the moon or stars for navigation, yet even species that do not wander far are also disorientated by light.[19]

An alternative explanation is that invisible electromagnetic waves at both the infrared and ultraviolet ends of the spectrum might also induce behavioural effects. The American entomologist Philip Callahan has suggested that candles emit similar infrared light frequencies to the luminescence of sex pheromones: the preponderance of male moths caught at light traps offers some credence to this suggestion, although males tend to be more active anyway at night. In essence, argues Callahan, the male moth dies 'trying to mate with the candle moth', in a curious scientific explanation for the poetic symbolism of the deadly attraction of moths to light.[20] He further suggests that artificial light sources such as street lamps have the effect of irradiating the chemical luminescence of pheromones, increasing their effect:

Any irradiated scent under the lamp will certainly emit at a much higher energy level than a scent pumped by night sky

K. A. Doktor-Sargent, *A moth trap in the woods*, c. 1976, drawing.

light. The attraction will be stronger to the lamp irradiated scent. The street light, like the candle, is a flickering modulated mimic of what occurs in nature under natural sky light conditions.[21]

Other entomologists, however, remain unconvinced since the ultraviolet spectrum is much more attractive to moths than the infrared spectrum, so this theory can, at best, offer only a partial explanation for moths' attraction to light.[22]

A third theory, the open-space theory advanced by the Russian entomologist Georgii Mazokhin-Porshnyakov, suggests that nocturnal moths seeking to fly out from the cover of vegetation will reach for the night sky as the brightest source of light. However, artificial sources of illumination are easily mistaken for this, and once caught in their glare, the moth is dazzled and disoriented. Losing its capacity for night vision, it rapidly becomes a 'prisoner of the lamp'. However, although the night sky predominantly emits short-wave luminescence similar to the ultraviolet spectrum which has long been known to have a powerful effect on moths, there is little resemblance between the diffuse illumination of the open sky and concentrated individual sources of artificial light.[23]

Finally, the Mach band hypothesis, named after the physiological studies of vision by the Austrian physicist Ernst Mach, suggests that moths actually seek to avoid light but that their eyes become disoriented by the contrast between a brightly lit focal point and the surrounding darkness.[24] The erratic flight paths of moths in the vicinity of light have been used to support this hypothesis, as they seem to indicate that moths are both attracted and repelled at the same time. Other oddities include different types of flight behaviours at successively closer distances to light, ranging from swerving lines of flight to rapidly descending, zigzag movements.

Furthermore, it appears that many moths in the vicinity of light do seek out nearby sources of darkness (as evidenced by the effectiveness of empty egg boxes inside moth traps where moths will readily seek out shelter).

There is growing evidence that light pollution is having a deleterious effect on the nocturnal ecology of moths and other organisms. The global scale of light pollution is steadily increasing with the development of new road networks, an increasing emphasis on 'night time economies' and changing perceptions of urban space in terms of expectations for higher levels of nocturnal illumination.[25] The German lepidopterist Axel Hausmann has estimated that huge numbers of moths are killed by car headlights and the intense glare and heat of floodlighting

White-lined hawkmoth, *Hyles lineata*, found under a streetlight in downtown Los Angeles, 2013.

used for sports stadia and other kinds of brightly lit buildings.[26] The nocturnal glow of industrial installations can also exert a heavy toll: early twentieth-century descriptions of the Scunthorpe iron works in Lincolnshire described how 'hundreds of thousands of moths perish annually by being drawn by the glare of Scunthorpe lights to destruction above the molten metal.'[27] Swarms of moths and other nocturnal insects attracted by floodlights can even disrupt sporting events, as witnessed at the Sydney Olympics of 2000, where a Noctuid moth called the Bogong, *Agrotis infusa*, was attracted in huge numbers:

> Bogongs appear to have been causing havoc ever since Europeans arrived in Australia. Records show that they invaded a Sydney church in 1865, forcing a service to be abandoned. In the mid-1970s, they swarmed into a new, brightly lit building in Canberra in such numbers that the lifts stopped working. More recently, the moths were un-invited guests at the 2000 Sydney Olympics, where they dive-bombed performers and athletes, even perching on Yvonne Kenny, the celebrated soprano, as she sang during the closing ceremony.[28]

The concern with moths killed by lights is reflected in the American film-maker Stan Brakhage's four-minute, 16-mm experimental work *Mothlight* (1963), comprised from a sequence of moth wings, leaves, petals and other fragments of dead insects. The idea for the film came from a sense of anxiety that Brakhage experienced upon seeing moths kill themselves on candles and lights: by collecting the wings of dead moths he wanted to create a work that would bring them back to life. The materials were placed between two strips of 16-mm splicing tape that were then contact printed in a lab to allow its cinematic projection.[29]

Stan Brakhage, *Mothlight* (1963). Courtesy of the Estate of Stan Brakhage.

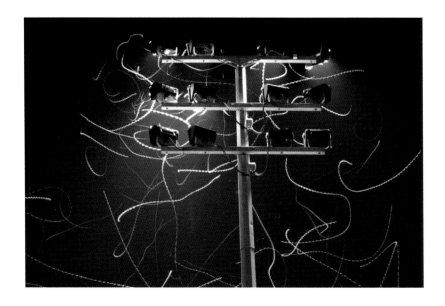

The attraction of moths to artificial light also inspired the American artist Ven Voisey, whose installation *Flutter* (*60 cycle Lamentation*) from 2004 comprised a 'one-note requiem' played on a violin accompanied by the amplified hum of fluorescent ceiling lights (above which small blurry shapes of cut-out moths could be seen). Photographers have also been intrigued by the strange trails left by moths flying around streetlights that can be produced by time-lapse exposures. And observers of searchlights have marvelled at the hugely magnified shapes passing through the beam.

The association between moths and light is both a cultural and ecological phenomenon. It is also a relationship that continues to puzzle scientists, along with many other dimensions to the lives of moths. Without their attraction to light we would know even less about their world and many species would be seldom seen at all. Yet the growing ubiquity of light – including ever more powerful forms of artificial illumination – poses real threats to the sustenance of their nocturnal realm.

5 Visitations

Every association of moths is with night and mystery and
death.
Donald Culross Peattie[1]

Moths, butterflies and other insects appear sparingly in the art
and symbolism of the Egyptian (c. 3050–332 BCE) and Minoan
(2700–1500 BCE) civilizations, and there are limited traces of their
presence in earlier Neolithic cultural artefacts from eastern China.
For ancient cultures of more lush regions, however – where there
is a greater profusion of brightly coloured insects – such as the
pre-Columbian cultures of the Inca, Maya and Zapotec, there are
numerous representations of butterflies and moths in art, architecture and folklore. Examples include the murals and painted
braziers found at the site of Teotihuacán (c. 100 BCE–700 CE) located
in present-day Mexico City.[2] In classical antiquity we can also find
occasional images of butterflies and moths: insects sometimes appear
on coins or tombs, for example, and one of the Pompeii frescoes
depicts an imaginary winged insect perched on a wheel of fortune
along with a skull and level to signify that all becomes equal through
death.

After the collapse of the Roman Empire the cultural
representation of butterflies and moths became much less frequent
in European culture. By the fourteenth century, however, insects
began to reappear, in the decorative margins of illuminated
manuscripts such as the Book of Hours and the Breviary, culminating in the exquisitely detailed works of the French miniaturist
Jean Bourdichon (c. 1457–1521).[3] So intricate are Bourdichon's works,

Memento mori
mosaic, Pompeii,
c. 1st century CE.

Jean Bourdichon,
*Les Grandes heures
d'Anne de Bretagne*
(1503–8).

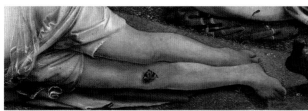

Piero di Cosimo, *Venus, Mars and Cupid*, 1505, and detail of moth on Venus's leg.

such as *Les Grandes heures d'Anne de Bretagne* (1503–8), that we can identify several species of moths and their caterpillars.

During the early sixteenth century moths and other insects begin to make more frequent appearances in art. Depictions of nature in this period range from nascent forms of landscape painting, often accompanying mythical or religious scenes, to still-life compositions. An example of this mix of genres is the work of the Italian Renaissance painter Piero di Cosimo (*c.* 1462–1521), who was clearly influenced by early Dutch landscape painters: his *Venus, Mars and Cupid* (1505) shows these mythological figures in a surprisingly conjugal setting, resting in an idyllic landscape, surrounded by rabbits, birds and even a brightly coloured moth that rests on the leg of Venus. The degree of entomological detail enables us to identify the insect as *Euplagia quadripunctaria* (known as *la falena dell'edera* in Italian or the Jersey Tiger in English). The presence of this pretty moth may suggest the fragility of life, or it may even be a gaudy portent of death – the worm in the apple has emerged in fancy dress – or perhaps di Cosimo simply borrowed the symbolic motif of a moth as the pretext to explore his fascination with the natural world. We shall never know for sure but the accuracy of the painting points towards the role of art in the early modern emergence of natural history.

During the seventeenth century the depiction of insects in still-life is developed further, especially in the Netherlands, as reflected in the work of Adriaen Coorte, Jan van Huysum, Daniel Seghers and Balthasar van der Ast. The representation of everyday objects reflected the tastes of a newly wealthy mercantile elite, with emphasis on themes of domestic well-being and personal possessions. These compositions are not entirely shorn of earlier cultural or symbolic associations, but they connect with growing aesthetic and scientific interest in accurate depictions of nature. With the work of the Flemish still-life painter Jan van Kessel (1626–1679), the focus on natural history becomes more direct, and we enter the realm of scientific illustration in the pre-Linnaean era. In van Kessel's *Stilleven van insecten en vruchten* (*c.* 1660–65), for example, three species of Lepidoptera are easily identifiable: the Speckled Wood butterfly, *Pararge aegeria*, the Cream-spot Tiger, *Arctia villica*, and the Magpie Moth, *Abraxas grossulariata*, along with its caterpillar correctly shown on gooseberry, one of its larval foodplants. As in the case of Maria Sibylla Merian's work (see Chapter Three), the emphasis is on the form and habits of living insects rather than the arrangement of set specimens derived from collections. Here, we encounter a mode of representation that is increasingly removed from allegorical motifs and focused on the visual attributes of natural history as an aesthetically mediated focus for scientific curiosity.[4]

Most literary evocations of moths before the modern era have focused on their attraction to light, but by the eighteenth century we can begin to detect other influences, with a renewed emphasis on folklore and myth associated with the rise of European romanticisms. In European folklore, for example, white moths were considered to be the souls of the dead, and this may be the origin of the vernacular name for *Hepialus humuli*, the Ghost Moth, whose white-winged males hover at dusk over moors, heaths and other grassy places.[5] It is likely that the Ghost Moth is among those species evoked in the final passage of Emily Brontë's *Wuthering Heights* (1847):

I lingered round them, under that benign sky: watched the moths fluttering among the heath and harebells; listened

Jan van Kessel, *Stilleven van insecten en vruchten*, *c.* 1660–65.

to the soft wind breathing through the grass, and wondered how anyone could ever imagine unquiet slumbers for the sleepers in that quiet earth.[6]

Although the narrator, Lockwood, is standing by the graves of Catherine, Heathcliff and Edgar, in an otherwise desolate place, the presence of life amid death is powerfully evoked, as well as perhaps a sense of nature's indifference to human suffering. This final passage of the novel is also the symbolic focal point for Andrea Arnold's cinematic adaptation of *Wuthering Heights,* released in 2011, where she uses moorland moths to lend the film a degree of entomological verisimilitude.[7]

Moths play a significant role in the literature of Virginia Woolf, whose family were avid natural history enthusiasts. For Woolf, moths evoke a feeling of mystery and suspense stirred by 'that pleasant sense of dark autumn nights and ivy-blossom'.[8] Through her childhood moth-hunting excursions, she became acutely aware of the magical transition from day into night. In her brief essay entitled 'Reading', written in 1919, she recalls the moment at dusk when the adults – who could no longer see properly – went back into the house, whereupon her adventure began:

Then, as they passed inside, the moths came out, the swift grey moths of the dusk, that only visit flowers for a second, never settling, but hanging an inch or two above the yellow of the evening primrose, vibrating to a blur. It was, I suppose, time to go into the woods.[9]

For Woolf, moths form part of the 'chaos and tumult of night' revealed through the shared excitement of moth hunting.[10] The technique she describes in this essay is called 'sugaring' in which various concoctions of beer, molasses, rum and other

sweet liquids are strategically applied to tree trunks and wood-
en posts before dusk.

> The road that skirted the wood was so pale that its hard-
> ness grated upon our boots unexpectedly. It was the last
> strip of reality, however, off which we stepped into the
> gloom of the unknown. The lantern shoved its wedge of
> light through the dark, as though the air were a fine black
> snow piling itself up in banks on either side of the yellow
> beam.[11]

After they enter the wood Woolf observes the strange behaviour
of insects attracted to their lantern after they place it on the ground.
They could hear 'little crackling sounds which seemed connected
with a slight waving and bending in the surrounding grass' as
various insects advanced towards the light. 'Their movements,'
writes Woolf, 'were all so awkward that they made one think of
sea creatures crawling on the floor of the sea.'[12] The nocturnal world
of these insects, now somehow compelled towards their light, has
been distorted by their lantern with its beam of light amid the
rustling darkness. Woolf and her small band of moth-hunters
cautiously approach the trees with growing excitement to see if
there are any visitors to their sugar:

> These lumps seemed unspeakably precious, too deeply
> attached to the liquid to be disturbed. Their proboscis were
> deep plunged, and as they drew in the sweetness, their wings
> quivered slightly as if in ecstasy. Even when the light was full
> upon them they could not tear themselves away, but sat there,
> quivering a little more uneasily perhaps, but allowing us to
> examine the tracery on the upper wing, those stains, spots,
> and veinings by which we decided their fate.[13]

And then suddenly they came upon the real object of their desire, one of the spectacular red underwings, its eyes glowing in the dark:

> Cautiously shielding the light, we saw from far off the glow of two red lamps which faded as the light turned upon them; and there emerged the splendid body which wore those two red lamps at its head. Great underwings of glowing crimson were displayed. He was almost still, as if he had alighted with his wing open and had fallen into a trance of pleasure. He seemed to stretch across the tree, and beside him other moths looked only like little lumps and knobs on the bark. He was splendid to look upon and so immobile that perhaps we were reluctant to end him; and yet when, as if guessing our intention and resuming a flight that had been temporarily interrupted, he roamed away, it seemed as if we had lost a possession of infinite value. Somebody cried out sharply. The lantern bearer flashed his light in the direction which the moth had taken.[14]

They continue the search for their elusive quarry, now venturing to the most distant tree that they had sugared earlier in the evening. Managing to capture their crimson prize and place it in their 'poison pot', their sense of triumph is disturbed, however, by 'a hollow rattle of sound in the deep silence of the wood which had I know not what of mournful and ominous about it':

> It waned and spread through the forest: it died away, then another of those deep sighs arose. An enormous silence succeeded. 'A tree,' we said at last. A tree had fallen.[15]

Woolf is clearly troubled by the capture of the magnificent moth and its death seems somehow connected with the distant sound

THE DEATH of THE MOTH

VIRGINIA WOOLF

Drawing by Vanessa Bell for the cover of Virginia Woolf's essay collection *The Death of the Moth* (1942).

of a falling tree. There is an implicit vitalist strand in Woolf's writing that finds an interconnectedness in the life force of nature. In her essay from the same year entitled 'The Death of the Moth', Woolf observes the struggle of a 'little hay-coloured moth' trapped behind a windowpane. She reflects on the desperate struggle of 'a tiny bead of pure life' against the greater force of death.[16] Her essay was composed against the background of colossal loss of life in the First World War, and may be read as an allegory for the distant carnage of war belied by the peaceful tranquility of the Sussex countryside:

The same energy which inspired the rooks, the ploughmen, the horses, and even, it seemed, the lean bare-backed downs, sent the moth fluttering from side to side of his square of the window pane . . . Watching him, it seemed as if a fibre, very thin but pure, of the enormous energy of the world had been thrust into his frail and diminutive body. As often as he crossed the pane, I could fancy that a thread of vital light became visible. He was little or nothing but life.[17]

Moths are also present in Woolf's landmark novel *The Waves* (1931), which evolved from a set of notes initially called 'The Moths', and her eventual choice of title may even be an oblique reference to a group of Geometrid moths known as 'waves', which Woolf would certainly have been familiar with (especially from leafing through the copy of Francis Orpen Morris's *British Moths* held in the family library).[18] Motifs drawn from nature are ever present in the novel. At one point the character Susan suggests that Rhoda's eyes 'are like those pale flowers to which moths come in the evening'.[19] Elsewhere in Woolf's writing the presence of moths is given an erotic charge as in the 'hum' of attraction played out in *Jacob's Room* (1922), where she compares Jacob Flanders's awakening sexuality to the hovering presence of a hawk-moth.[20]

The German émigré and writer W. G. Sebald had several moth books in his library, including *British Sphinxes* (1936) and the popular German identification guide *Heimische Nachtfalter nach Farbfotos erkannt* (1993).[21] For Sebald, moths reveal a secret world of complexity, with their menagerie of strange names, intricate patterns and singular life histories. He is intrigued by their apparent invisibility until they reveal themselves at night swirling around lights, leaving a 'phantom trace' for the human eye that is nothing more than a trick of the light, like distant stars.[22] Sebald's long-standing fascination with moths not only evokes childhood memories but connects with his reflections on loss, memory and the mysteries of non-human sentience.[23] In his final novel, *Austerlitz* (2001), framed around a friendship between a narrator (loosely based on the author himself) and the character Austerlitz, there are several detailed and nuanced references to moths. Austerlitz recalls being taken on a moth-hunting expedition at night by his great-uncle Alphonso, 'to spend a few hours looking into the mysterious world of moths':

Soon after darkness fell we were sitting on a promontory far above Andromeda Lodge, behind us the higher slopes and before us the immense darkness out at sea, and no sooner had Alphonso placed his incandescent lamp in a shallow hollow surrounded by heather and lit it than the moths, not one of which we had seen during our climb, came flying in as if from nowhere, describing thousands of arcs and spirals and loops, until like snowflakes they formed a silent swarm around the light, while others, wings whirring, crawled over the sheet spread under the lamp or else, exhausted by their wild circling, settled in the grey recesses of the egg boxes stacked in a crate by Alphonso to provide shelter for them.[24]

There is something mysterious for Sebald about not only their strange habits but their mode of being. By day moths seem to exist in a state of torpor, as they sit motionless near the lights or windows that had drawn them in the night before, resting patiently, 'even after death, held fast by the tiny claws that stiffened in their last agony'. Sebald reflects on the mysteries of the moth's inner world. 'and who knows, said Austerlitz, perhaps moths dream as well, perhaps a lettuce in the garden dreams as it looks up at the moon by night.'[25]

Sebald is intrigued by the presence of moths within modernity. In a poignant passage towards the end of *Austerlitz*, the eponymous character reflects on an Ashkenazi Jewish cemetery near his home in Stepney, East London. He wonders whether this overgrown cemetery, dating from the eighteenth century, is the origin of the moths that regularly enter his house:

> there was a plot where lime trees and lilacs grew and in which members of the Ashkenazi community had been buried since the eighteenth century . . . He had discovered the cemetery, from which, as he now suspected, the moths used to fly into his house, said Austerlitz, only a few days before he left London, when the gate in the wall stood open for the first time in all the years he had lived in Alderney Street.[26]

For Sebald, the Ashkenazi cemetery serves as a site of hidden memories within the heart of the city; in European cities in the post-war era many Jewish cemeteries fell into a state of abandonment and disorder because the relatives who might have tended graves or contributed towards their upkeep had perished in the Holocaust. These neglected spaces had become transformed into tranquil islands of nature within the city, in an uncanny contrast with those distant places of barbarity that had contributed to their formation.

The moth that has had the closest association with mystery and death is undoubtedly the Death's-head Hawk-moth. There are in fact two other closely related species, *A. lachesis* and *A. styx*, but it is the European death's-head that has been the most intense focus of attention, especially in northern Europe where its appearance is more sporadic. The French scientist René-Antoine Ferchault de Réaumur describes in his *Mémoires pour servir à l'histoire des insectes*

(1734–42) how the people of Brittany feared the Death's-head Hawk-moth as 'a certain harbinger of epidemic illnesses and pestilences' with its wings resembling mortuary drapes. In Hungary, it was believed that if this moth entered the home then a death in the family would follow, while even contact with a single scale has been feared in parts of rural France as a cause of blindness.[27] In Germany, the moth's squeaking sound, which it emits if distressed, was considered to be 'the audible warning of the approach of death itself', and this strange sound is also referred to by the Italian poet Guido Gozzano (1883–c. 1916) as the cry of the damned.[28] The 'death-moth' is also present in the first stanza of John Keats's 'Ode on Melancholy' (1819):

> No, no, go not to Lethe, neither twist
>   Wolf's-bane, tight-rooted, for its poisonous wine;
> Nor suffer thy pale forehead to be kiss'd
>   By nightshade, ruby grape of Proserpine;
>   Make not your rosary of yew-berries,
>   Nor let the beetle, nor the death-moth be
>   Your mournful Psyche, nor the downy owl
> A partner in your sorrow's mysteries;
>   For shade to shade will come too drowsily,
>   And drown the wakeful anguish of the soul.[29]

It is this moth that plays the role of the 'sphinx' in Edgar Allan Poe's short story by the same name. The tale is set 'during the dread reign of cholera in New York' and was published in 1846 just three years before the author's death. The narrator of the story decides to take a two-week sojourn in a cottage to escape the ill-health of the city. One evening, however, as he looks out onto the landscape of the Hudson Valley, he beholds a 'living monster of hideous conformation, which very rapidly made its way from the summit to the bottom, disappearing finally in the dense forest below'. Doubting his own sanity he checks the apparition in a natural history volume, but the 'monster' turns out to be an optical distortion created by a moth caught in a cobweb that has become grossly magnified in his line of sight as if it is hovering over the landscape.[30]

The moth is depicted in William Holman Hunt's Pre-Raphaelite painting *The Hireling Shepherd* (1851), in which the errant shepherd shows a young woman a Death's-head Hawk-moth, as his flock begins to wander in the background. In this instance the presence of the moth seems to indicate a pastoral scene that is drifting awry: when Hunt first exhibited the painting he included a few lines from Shakespeare's *King Lear* about a foolish shepherd and his beguiling 'minikin mouth' and he may also have been influenced by John Milton's *Amaryllis* (a theme that Hunt developed directly in another work) along with the languid pastoral scenes of François Boucher.[31]

The Death's-head Hawk-moth is used in Luis Buñuel and Salvador Dalí's eerie and dream-like film *Un Chien Andalou* (1929) (although the moth is clearly a dead specimen stuck to a wall) and in Yasujirō Ozu's *Tokyo Story* (1953) where a hawk-moth flutters around a lamp to signify that the mother is dying (suggesting that this symbolic association with death extends beyond Europe). Perhaps the most disturbing recent cinematic use of the death's-head hawk-moth is in Jonathan Demme's *The Silence of the Lambs* (1991), where it is left in the throat of a young female victim of a serial killer being pursued by FBI agent Clarice Starling (played by Jodie Foster). Yet Demme's use of the Death's-head has been criticized for its entomological inaccuracies: the pupa extracted from the victim's throat is actually that of the Tobacco Sphinx or Goliath Worm, *Manduca sexta*, but with a false 'death's-head' pattern artificially attached. The 'real' Death's-head Hawk-moth

is absent from North America and the transport of live moths from Europe would have proved problematic: as a consequence Demme's film made use of 'stand-in' moths bred in a laboratory in South Carolina, transported in a special-purpose, permanently illuminated container to prevent them from flying around and damaging their wings. In the poster for the film the death's-head pattern on the thorax of the moth is replaced with a photograph by Philippe Halsman, made in collaboration with Salvador Dalí, entitled *In Voluptas Mors* (Voluptuous Death, 1951), depicting Dalí alongside seven naked models arranged in the shape of a human skull as a 'tableau vivant'.[32]

In Peter Greenaway's film *Drowning by Numbers* (1988), moths are a connecting thread throughout the movie, which is divided into 100 parts in a curious tale of enumeration, classification and duplicity. In part two, a couple of Angle Shades, *Phlogophora*

William Holman Hunt, *The Hireling Shepherd*, 1851, oil on canvas.

An image from Luis Buñuel and Salvador Dalí's *Un Chien Andalou* (1929).

John Heartfield, *Metamorphose* (1934). The metamorphosis of the Death's-head Hawk-moth as political metaphor for the rise of Nazism.

Poster for Jonathan Demme's *The Silence of the Lambs* (1991), designed by Dawn Baillie.

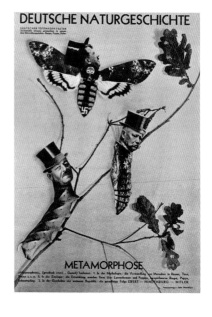

Philippe Halsman,
In Voluptas Mors,
1951.

meticulosa, a Barred Sallow, *Xanthia aurago*, and various other autumnal insects wander over fruit laid out in a still-life composition based on the iconography of seventeenth-century Dutch art. Moments later we encounter a Death's-head Hawk-moth on a wall (a set specimen in an apparent reference to *Un Chien Andalou*). In sequence 39 the local coroner Madgett (played by Bernard Hill) and his son Smut (Jason Edwards) go moth-catching in the woods where they find a pair of Elephant Hawk-moths, *Deilephila elpenor*, which they dutifully compare with an illustration from the classic eighteenth-century plate in Moses Harris's *Aurelian*.

Moths also appear in contemporary art. The installation *Black Cloud* (2007), by the Mexican artist Carlos Amorales, first shown at New York's Yvon Lambert Gallery, consists of 25,000 black paper moths hand-glued to the walls and ceiling of the gallery. This large-scale installation looms over the viewer as a kind of ominous infestation. In a recent interview Amorales relates the work to the memory of his grandmother and his childhood experiences of nature, the possibility that something beautiful can become disquieting en masse, and the idea of the social insect as a kind of single organism or one interconnected body.[33]

In other cases the swarm motif has been replaced with ordered arrangements reminiscent of museum displays or entomological cabinets. The British artist Damien Hirst, as part of his 'Entomology series' begun in 2009, has developed works based on the display of dead insects, with titles such as *Inferno* and *Purgatorio* (both 2009) making reference to Dante's *Divine Comedy*. The compositions play on the dual purpose of insect collections as scientific compendiums and elaborate forms of display with particular emphasis on the role of symmetry in nature. For his retrospective held at the Tate Modern in 2012, Hirst used thousands of live butterflies along with a 'brand tie-up' with the fashion designer Alexander McQueen for a series of luxury scarves (following an earlier entomological collaboration between Hirst and Prada for the design of handbags). In these (and other) works Hirst uses elements of nature in a synthesis between art and capitalism. The installations and their design spin-offs serve as an aesthetic corollary to the commodification of nature that imperils biodiversity, yet these connections are ignored by both the artist and the institutional nexus that provides credence for his work.

Moths form part of a gothic sensibility, ranging from macabre novels to heavy metal insignia, but only a few species regularly feature in this context, such as the Luna Moth, *Actias luna*, a North American kind of silk moth, which serves as a symbol of mystery and aesthetic perfection, and the Death's-head Hawk-moth, with its long-standing association with death, ill omen or occult fantasies. These two species remain the most popular choice of 'real' moths for modern tattoos and body adornment. Moths also have a subcultural presence in graffiti art. Hawk-moths and Moon Moths feature prominently, especially in wall paintings with gothic sources of inspiration, but other more enigmatic representations can be found. The interior of an abandoned building in post-industrial Sheffield in the north of England even briefly had an unmistakable Oleander Hawk-moth, *Daphnis nerii*, with its rich swirl of green markings almost

Carlos Amorales's installation *Black Cloud* at the Museum Kunst der Westküste, Germany, 2009.

Album cover by James Marsh for Talk Talk's *The Colour of Spring* (1986).

perfectly suited for spray-can art, before its summary demolition. In the coastal town of Hastings in East Sussex we encounter the *Hastings Moth Project*, dating from 2013, devised by the art collective zeroh, which resembles a series of stencil-based graffiti tags but is in fact a public art project which mimics street art, using the theme of insect metamorphosis to symbolize economic regeneration.[34]

Moths have also adorned album cover artwork. The Canadian artist Benjamin Vierling's painting for the Joanna Newsom album *YS* (2006) depicts the singer in the style of seventeenth-century portraiture, in which the sitter was often accompanied by natural history artefacts or other favourite possessions. In this case the Dun-bar, *Cosmia trapezina*, is presented to the viewer as a set specimen, held in Newsom's hand. The art deco influence of the French artist and entomologist Eugène Séguy can also be discerned in the artwork for the English band Talk Talk, and in particular their album *The Colour of Spring* (1986) designed by James Marsh. Other examples of decorative arts using moths include the Australian artist Deborah Klein's *Moth Masks* series (2007–13), where masks are used to emphasize both the individuality and unknowability of each human–moth subject. Each of the paintings is named after the scientific name of the species shown, and the project has recently been extended to include painted masks held in wooden cabinets similar to those used in entomological collections.

The cultural presence of moths remains intriguing and perplexing. The nineteenth-century efflorescence of gothic and romantic depictions of moths remains very present through contemporary manifestations ranging from cinema and fiction to subcultural motifs adorning the surfaces of walls or even the human body itself. The moth, as a cultural symbol of the night, retains long-standing popular associations with mystery and

Album cover by Benjamin A. Vierling for Joanna Newsom's *YS* (2006).

darkness, but it also connects with questions of memory, non-human sentience and even vitalist reflections on the inter-connectedness of life.

Deborah Klein
Argina astrea,
2007, from the
Moth Masks series
(2007–9).

6 Any Colour You Like

And diamonded with panes of quaint device,
Innumerable of stains and splendid dyes,
As are the tiger-moth's deep damask'd wings
John Keats[1]

In his poem 'The Eve of St Agnes' (1819) John Keats compares the colours of a Tiger Moth with the translucent brilliance of stained glass. Keats depicts the interface between art and nature through an intricately patterned moth wing that 'both naturalizes art and aestheticizes nature'.[2] Unlike the tactile and olfactory realm of plants, we find that the human experience of moths resides largely in the narrower sensory field of vision alone. This avowedly ocularcentrist universe poses an acute dilemma, since the challenge of colour exceeds merely diagrammatic modes of representation and the 'vaunted objectivity' of the natural sciences.[3] The diversity of colour in nature lies at the limits of both scientific knowledge and human attempts at its cultural representation.

What evolutionary processes could have led to such an extraordinary range of colours and patterns in moths: not just green, orange, blue and red in every shade, but even metallic inscriptions of silver and gold? The origins of the intricate polychromatic universe that Keats and other writers have so vividly described most probably lie in the evolution of insects and their adoption of various aposematic (warning) patterns and co-evolutionary relationships with the pollination needs of flowering plants. Phylogenetic analysis of insect eyes, including the Lepidoptera, shows that the evolution of photosensitive pigments called 'opsins' occurred at an early stage, meaning that invertebrates were among the first organisms to

The spectacular Geometrid moth *Eucyclodes gavissima* is found in South and East Asia.

develop sophisticated colour vision.[4] The evolutionary pressures promoting both the existence and perception of colour must have been intense: day-flying insects needed to see each other, but not be eaten, and flowers in turn needed to be noticed in order to be pollinated.

A particular challenge for entomological illustrators was how to represent the vibrant colours of living moths in contrast with dead specimens held in collections. Vivid greens, for example, usually faded to a dull yellow, and in some cases only 'interference' colours created by the structural characteristics of wing scales remained significantly unchanged. The English naturalist Moses Harris was especially interested in how visual effects observed in nature could be recreated in illustrated books and produced the first 'colour wheel' using the colour theory of Isaac Newton, whose influential *Optics* (1704) had shown, using a prism, that colour was a product of light, and therefore a matter of perception rather than an intrinsic property of objects.[5]

Colour comprises different 'registers' or systems of perception that operate in combination: there are 'natural colours' including

Pl. 14

the chemical properties of pigments, the refractive effects of crystals, and other measurable determinants of colour as a material field; there are subjective dimensions to the experience of colour (including individual differences in the ability to perceive colours); and there are iconographic characteristics of colour associated with cultural and historical context.[6] Human aesthetic experience of colour in nature is not reducible to the physical properties of colour alone, or to subjective differences in perception or prevailing conceptions of 'beauty', but by an interweaving between these different elements.

Although Keats's paean to the tiger moth is very much in the romantic tradition, with an emphasis on colour and light, we can move beyond this frame by emphasizing how the pigmentation

Peggy Macnamara, *Illinois Insects*, 2005.

Emile-Alain (Eugène) Séguy, *Papillons* (1928).

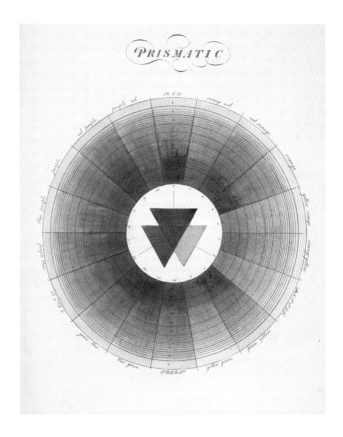

has a clear aposematic (warning) function in ecology, quite independent of our ability to perceive these colours or patterns. Our subjective response to brightly coloured insects stems not just from variations in ability to perceive colour but also from the cultures of nature that have developed in relation to the aesthetic appreciation of individual organisms. Tiger moths, like those evoked by Keats, were among the earliest insects to be depicted in art, not just because of their striking colours or 'lazy flight' (they have little fear of predators) but because their ornate appearance resonated with existing conceptions of beauty in nature.

The wings of Lepidoptera owe their colours and patterns to thousands of tiny scales that originally evolved from protective hairs in a similar fashion to fish scales or bird feathers.[7] These scales produce a vivid array of colours and visual effects through three main mechanisms: defraction, interference and the scattering of light. The colour white, for example, is created by the structural characteristics of wing scales that scatter light in all directions or by specific pigments such as pterins. Many 'structural colours' such as silver, gold or iridescent blues or greens are produced by tiny differences in the arrangement or shape of scales.[8] The pigment-based colours are either produced by the insect itself as it undergoes metamorphosis or derived from chemicals in plants eaten by the caterpillar such as flavonoids (which create various shades of white or yellow).

Around six or seven different classes of pigments in Lepidoptera have been recognized so far, but there are undoubtedly others yet to be identified. The melanins producing black colouration, for

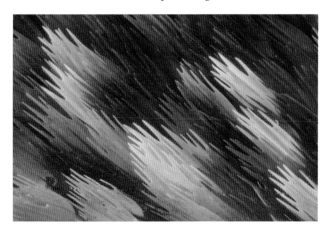

Magnified scales on the wing of the Comet Moth by Linden Gledhill.

example, are highly varied and not well understood.[9] Black has a curious place within the colour range of moths, and its function is not always clear. There are alpine or boreal day-flying species that are dark so that they can absorb solar radiation, but not all black species fit into this thermal explanation: the jet black Chimney Sweeper, *Odezia atrata*, for example, flies in warm sunshine at lower altitudes and hardly ventures from pignut, *Conopodium majus*, the herb on which its caterpillars feed.

As the wings form inside the pupa, waves of different pigments are released through the insect's haemolymph (the arthropod equivalent of blood) to affect only the scales destined to bear that colour.[10] Analysis of wing patterns has suggested that there is a basic model around which a huge variety of final outcomes have evolved. The wings of Lepidoptera represent an almost infinite evolutionary canvas, or 'morphospace', in the face of external pressures. Specific

Magnified scales on the wing of the Madagascan Sunset Moth by Linden Gledhill.

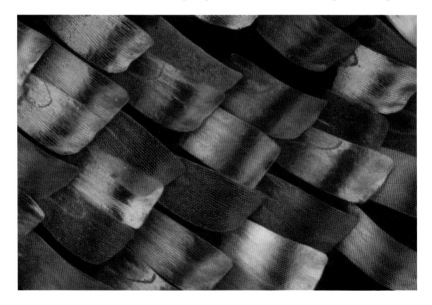

A recently emerged Comet Moth, *Argema mittrei*, drying its wings in forest understory, Andasibe-Mantadia National Park, Madagascar.

morphogens have been identified that can activate switches for particular colour genes along with the presence of nodal points or 'organizational centres' that enable eyespots and other more complex patterns to be created.[11]

So beguiling are the wings of Lepidoptera that artists have used them to produce collages, recreating the pixelated or pointillist arrangement of scales at a larger scale for visual effect. The French artist Jean Dubuffet, for example, created intricate two-dimensional patterns with wings, including composite human figures or faces that are reminiscent of the 'vegetable faces' of the Italian mannerist painter Giuseppe Arcimboldo (1527–93). Works such as *Le Strabique* (1953), *Nez d'Apollo Pap* (1953) and *Jardin Mouvementé* (1955) blur the distinction between organic and inorganic form. In a more abstract manner the wing patterns of moths have influenced the design of clothes, tapestries and other cultural artefacts. The Norwegian photographer Kjell B. Sandved, for example, has compared the details of a Noctuid wing with fabric design from sub-Saharan Africa. Sandved has also devised an 'alphabet' derived

from close-up photographs of the bizarre resemblances of wing markings with letters and numbers.

Jean Dubuffet, *Nez d'Apollo Pap*, 1953.

Is there an intersection between aesthetics and science in the field of entomology? The German biologist Ernst Haeckel (1834–1919) certainly thought so, believing that visually pleasing patterns held deeper clues to the evolutionary relationships between organisms. In a similar fashion to the earlier works of Maria Sibylla Merian, Haeckel used art as an investigative tool to emphasize the interconnectedness of life rather than restrict his focus on individual organisms.[12] The relationship between aesthetics and science has also been explored more recently by the philosopher Allen Carlson who suggests that a scientific understanding of nature can enrich our aesthetic appreciation of its complexities, interactions and even counter-intuitive elements such as decomposition.[13] To be fully immersed in the strange world of Tineid moths, for example, includes investigations of owl pellets, bracket fungi, rotten wood and even cadavers at an advanced stage

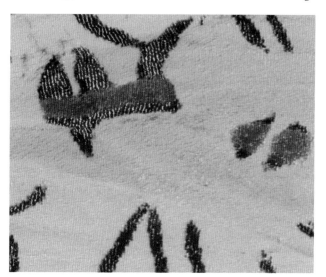

Kjell B. Sandved, detail of Noctuid wing, Congo (c. 1970s).

137

of decay. Nabokov similarly insisted that even the apparently dry art
of taxonomy should be seen in terms of visual pleasure, arguing that
the differentiation of species required meticulous attention to detail;
he delighted in the esoteric dimensions to taxonomy that paralleled
non-utilitarian dimensions to art and literature.[14]

Can we speak of a universal aesthetics of nature? The American biologist Edward O. Wilson suggests that humans possess an innate 'biophilia' or love of nature, though the idea that there are universal, culturally ubiquitous patterns of beauty in nature is difficult to establish.[15] It seems more likely that human aesthetic responses are never fully transcultural or transhistorical but always rooted in their cultural context. In any case, many of the colours or patterns that we might find attractive, such as the striking markings of tiger moths, are a signal of distaste or toxicity to other organisms.

To imagine the world of moths is to step outside the realm of human perception – if such an imaginative leap is possible – and encounter colours beyond our visible spectrum along with other kinds of sensory stimuli we can only guess at. The sensory world of moths is most probably a synaesthetic space in which the acoustic, haptic and olfactory realms are interwoven beyond the parameters of the merely visual. There is evidence, for example, that some pheromones emit visible wavelengths, so these may have multisensory behavioural effects. If we could step outside the limits of human vision, as Stan Brakhage has suggested, we would have to 'imagine a world alive with incomprehensible objects and shimmering with an endless variety of movement and innumerable gradations of color'.[16] To notice moths and make subtle visual differentiations between similar species or spot their cryptic patterns resting against the bark of trees is a process of unlearning the degree of sensory elimination that characterizes everyday life.

7 Pretenders

. . . he told me about these magic masks of mimicry; about the enormous moth which in a state of repose assumes the image of a snake looking at you; of a tropical geometrid coloured in perfect imitation of a species of butterfly infinitely removed from it in nature's system . . .
Vladimir Nabokov[1]

The life of a moth is fraught with danger at every stage of its life cycle. The co-evolutionary dynamics of moths and their predators has long been a source of cultural and scientific fascination. Moths have developed a remarkable diversity of survival strategies to fool, hide from or even ward off other animals that might want to eat them, including various kinds of crypsis (camouflage and other tactics to avoid being seen) and mimicry (resemblance to other species with similar or superior defences). The astonishing intricacy of these survival strategies has even provoked reflections on whether the degree of aesthetic, and even behavioural, perfection that these moths have achieved in imitating other organisms confounds the utilitarian basis of evolutionary theory.

Even eggs, the smallest and most inconspicuous stage in a moth's life cycle, are subject to predation. Despite the fact that they are often hidden (laid in bark crevices, under leaves, in the axils of stems) or protected by discarded hairs or web-like fragments of cocoons, these tiny beads of life are hunted down by small insects such as ants or targeted by parasitoid wasps that search by smell rather than by sight. It is at the caterpillar stage where moths begin to deploy the full diversity of protective strategies. Not only do birds consume huge quantities of caterpillars, especially in the spring in order to feed their young, but beetles, bugs, lizards and small mammals will eat them. Caterpillars are also susceptible to viral, bacterial or fungal attacks (except for the highly poisonous burnet caterpillars of the family Zygaenidae, which seem to repel even viruses). There are also some caterpillars, such as those of the Silky Wainscot, *Chilodes maritima*, that are known to attack each other, or caterpillars of other species, but instances of cannibalism are restricted to just a few species, and tend to occur in situations of food stress.

Among the most pervasive threats that caterpillars face are the relentless attacks of parasitoid wasps and flies. These predatory insects lay their eggs either in, on or near their prey, and their larvae then proceed to gradually devour their host, keeping them alive just long enough to provide sustenance. Such strategies have their logic: not only is the caterpillar kept 'fresh' but it continues to behave relatively normally so that its usual defences against larger predators such as birds protect the growing parasites within.[2] Many species of wasps are able to pierce the body of the caterpillar with a sharpened ovipositor, while parasitic flies generally lay their eggs on leaves that the unsuspecting caterpillar will ingest. Even underwater caterpillars such as those of the China-mark moths in the Crambidae family are not completely safe since there are wasps that can dive down to reach them.[3] Nor are caterpillars that are hidden inside the branches and trunks of trees safe: some wasps possess specialist drill-like ovipositors capable of cutting through wood to reach their prey.

It is a strange sight to see not a moth or butterfly emerging from a pupa but a menacing-looking wasp. Since these predators almost invariably kill their host they are referred to as 'parasitoids' to distinguish them from the relatively few 'true parasites' of Lepidopetera, such as mites, that live in less deadly relation with their host. So significant is this evolutionary relationship between moths and parasitoids that there are over 20,000 species of tachinid flies, over 40,000 species of braconid wasps, over 60,000 species of ichneumonid wasps, and more than 400,000 chalcidoid wasps, that prey on caterpillars.[4]

There is a progressive sequence in the eating habits of many parasitoids, which begins with less important tissues before finally devouring the key organs of their host (even more advanced animals such as toads are vulnerable to a similarly grisly fate). Among the ghoulish distinctions between these predators are the neatness of wasps versus the messiness of flies. However, we should not forget that many parasitoid larvae can themselves be targeted as hosts for yet smaller larvae of so-called 'hyper-parasites' (or 'secondary-parasitoids') so that the chain of predation is extended yet further.[5]

In his book *Creative Evolution* (1907) the French philosopher Henri Bergson draws on the earlier scientific observations of the entomologist Jean-Henri Fabre to discuss the troubling relationship between the parasitoid wasp of the genus *Ammophila* and its caterpillar prey. The wasp is able to paralyse its host with a series of clinically targeted stings to the main nerves passing through each segment of its body. Bergson wonders how a wasp can have such precise knowledge, and compares the understanding of its prey with that of the entomologist who can only know the caterpillar from the 'outside'. For Bergson, the 'hereditary transmission of contracted habit' is an insufficient explanation for the wasp's apparent intelligence. He therefore posits a different explanation based on the idea that 'caterpillar' and 'wasp' should be considered as relational activities rather than different organisms.[6]

For Bergson, the more distant working relationship between scientist and object of study compares badly with the skill of the wasp in relation to the caterpillar, which he ascribes to some kind of vital force or *élan vital* inherent to the natural world and not reducible to evolutionary genetics and the role of heredity in behaviour. While vitalist philosophy à la Bergson remains a highly contentious epistemological field, and is rejected by most modern biologists, the original observations of wasp behaviour by Fabre remain a source of fascination.[7]

Caterpillars are by no means passive in the face of these enemies. Hairiness is one defence mechanism, acting as a physical barrier to prevent eggs from being laid either in or on the caterpillar. Additionally, specialized types of hairs, such as extensible barbs laden with poison, may provide a further line of defence. As they grow in size some caterpillars develop various appendages that they can flail around like clubs or whips to fend off predators. To avoid olfactory detection caterpillars may also fling their droppings (known as 'frass') as far away as possible, thus putting would-be predators off the scent. Some caterpillars also have internal defences that enable them to isolate and destroy eggs or small larvae within their bodies, an action not dissimilar to that of antibodies that bind to threatening micro-organisms.[8] Parasitized caterpillars are also known to bask in the sun in order to use heat as a weapon against their internal intruders. Perhaps most astonishing of all, there is evidence that some caterpillars will self-medicate by chewing poisonous leaves in order to destroy the deadly parasitoids lurking within their bodies.[9]

To defend against larger predators that hunt by sight, many caterpillars have evolved mechanisms to avoid visual detection. Caterpillars from the Geometridae, or 'loopers', sometimes resemble thorns or broken twigs, resting motionless at an angle by day only to resume feeding by night. Kent's Geometer, *Selenia kentaria*, occurring in the forests of North America, is among the most intricate of the twig mimics, even growing subtle bark-like protuberances.[10] The caterpillar of the Showy Emerald, *Dichorda iridaria*, also found in North America, mimics dead leaves with a row of 'dorsolateral flanges' that resemble the plant on which it feeds:

Jewel caterpillar, *Acraga coa*, from the Dalceridae family, photographed in Mexico.

Caterpillar from the *Mahanta* genus of the Limacodidae (slug moths) with stinging hairs, from Pu'er, Yunnan, China.

OPPOSITE TOP
Caterpillar of the Spotted Apatelodes moth, *Apatelodes torrefacta*.

OPPOSITE BOTTOM
Caterpillar of the Flannel Moth, *Megalopyge opercularis*.

The caterpillar resembles a withered sumac leaflet. It may rest with the anterior portion of its body raised and looped or crooked to one side, adding to its guise as an aged, browning sumac leaflet. Emerald caterpillars have a single gear – slow. If disturbed, their caterpillars often quaver from side to side, much like loosely attached leaves being pushed about by a light breeze.[11]

In a similar fashion, the Blotched Emerald, *Comibaena bajularia*, a striking denizen of oak woods in temperate zones across much of Europe and eastwards to Japan, has a caterpillar that disguises itself by attaching fragments of leaves to its body so that it can creep along the stems of its foodplant unseen, not unlike the advancing trees of Birnam Wood in Shakespeare's *Macbeth*. In North America, there are several 'loopers' of the genus *Synchlora* that adorn their bodies with petals to become mobile flower mimics, leading the entomologist David L. Wagner to describe

The thorn mimic caterpillar of the Swallow-tailed Moth, *Ourapteryx sambucaria*, that intrigued Roger Caillois and other early 20th-century sceptics of Darwinian evolution.

The caterpillar of *Pygaera timon* tries to merge with the twig it is clinging to.

The caterpillar of the Blotched Emerald, *Comibaena bajularia*, attaches fragments of leaves to its body as a form of camouflage.

them as 'a Mardi Gras caterpillar that is out of costume only after
a molt'.[12]

Other caterpillars, such as the red underwings of the genus
Catocala, prefer to slink along crevices in bark or wrap their bodies
so tightly around stems that they are all but impossible to spot
(often aided by rows of 'shadow elimination hairs' that help them
to disappear from view). But if disturbed, some of these larger
Catocala caterpillars can switch to feigned attack mode by making
darting movements of their head that 'bump' potential predators
with pretend bites.[13] Other caterpillars, and even adult moths, will
also contort their bodies to reveal intersegmental rings that resemble
banded forms of warning colouration.

The caterpillars of the Elephant Hawk-moth, *Deilephila elpenor*,
will contract the front of their body to create a false head with eyes,
so they appear as snakes to predators. So intricate are these false
eyes that in some species they contain tiny white dots to resemble
light reflections. In other species this 'snake's head' can even pro-
trude a foul-smelling tongue-like protrusion, or the caterpillar may
use behavioural mimicry such as swaying its body from side to side
in a menacing way.

Another defence is for caterpillars to cluster together so that
they appear to be one much larger organism snaking its way
across tree trunks, vegetation or even open ground. The so-called
processionary moths, for example, adopt this strategy as they
move in formation in search of new sources of food. The young
larvae of the Buff-tip, *Phalera bucephala*, feed together gregariously
and, when disturbed, will all rear their heads simultaneously
until the danger has passed (the wing pattern of the similarly
ingenious adult moth enables it to disguise itself as a broken birch
twig).

One of the most remarkable caterpillar defence strategies of all
is that of Harris's Three-spot, *Harrisimemna trisignata*, a moth

The caterpillar of Harris's Three-spot, *Harrisimemna trisignata*, is among the most unappetizing-looking of all.

encountered in marshy woodlands from southern Canada to Florida and Texas. 'By almost any measure,' writes David L. Wagner, 'this is an exceptional animal – the caterpillar resembles a bird dropping, a pile of debris, a moldy cadaver, a spider, and who knows what else.' Among its more curious features the caterpillar retains the discarded head capsules from its previous moults, suspended on long hairs jutting out from behind its head, to create a kind of 'mace', which it thrashes against predators, batting away flies, wasps and other enemies in this manner. 'In addition,' notes Wagner, 'if molested, the caterpillar will rock its body with blurring rapidity – the effect is much like that of a spider rapidly tugging on its web (stabilimentum).'[14]

Instead of hiding, some caterpillars adopt a strategy of making themselves as conspicuous as possible with various forms of warning colouration against would-be predators. The striking black-and-yellow striped caterpillars of the Cinnabar moth, *Tyria jacobaeae*, for example, feed on the highly poisonous plant ragwort, *Senecio jacobaea*, and concentrate the alkaloid toxins in their bodies as a defence mechanism. In effect, the Cinnabar and many other distasteful moths have succeeded in unravelling the chemical defence strategies of plants and then using the acquired compounds for their own protection. This use of warning colouration is known as 'Müllerian mimicry' (named after the German biologist Fritz Müller): the appearance signals to predators that the caterpillar is unpalatable or poisonous and thus not worth eating.

The caterpillar of the Cinnabar moth, *Tyria jacobaeae*, concentrates toxins in its body from its larval foodplant and is an unpalatable Müllerian mimic with yellow- and black-banded warning colouration.

Some caterpillars deploy both crypsis and mimicry at different stages of their development. The caterpillar of the Alder Moth, *Acronicta alni*, resembles a bird dropping until its final moult when it is transformed into a brightly coloured black-and-yellow striped creature, complete with a set of black 'paddles' to flail at predators, although it is not poisonous and is therefore an example of 'Batesian mimicry', whereby a harmless organism resembles one that is best avoided. One possible reason for this switch in strategy adopted by the Alder Moth and many other species is that as the caterpillar grows in size it becomes more difficult to remain unseen, so there is a gradual or even sudden development of frightening protuberances, spikes, spines or other features.

Still more remarkable is the Hag Moth, *Phobetron pithecium*, also known as the Monkey Slug because of the curious shape of the caterpillar, found in orchards and woodlands from Quebec to Arkansas. This caterpillar has an extremely odd appearance: from above it resembles a strange kind of spider, a dead leaf furred with mould or, most probably, a discarded tarantula skin (although these spiders are absent from North America, the *Phobetron* genus is well represented south of Mexico). If turned upside down the caterpillar enhances its apparent unpalatability further by strange internal contortions of its abdomen, which make it appear as if a large *Alien*-like grub is squirming around within its body. If all these visual tricks should fail, a final line of defence is present in the shape of stinging hairs that can cause serious discomfort or irritation. As for the adult moth, the female looks like a bee, complete with yellow tufts on its legs resembling pollen baskets, while the male is a wasp mimic, so that we must contend with a moth that mimics several kinds of organisms or unpalatable objects at different stages of its life cycle.[15]

The greatest threat to adult moths that fly by night is bats. Many species have evolved specialized tympanal (hearing) organs that

The caterpillar of the Alder Moth, *Acronicta alni*, mimics bird droppings during its early instars. After its final moult the caterpillar is transformed into a dramatic yet harmless Batesian mimic with characteristic aposematic (warning) colouration.

The extraordinary caterpillar of *Phobetron hipparchia* is related to the Monkey Slug found in North America.

The caterpillars of the *Phobetron* genus are among the strangest of all, with weird appendages and contorted body shapes. This specimen was found in São Bernardo do Campo, São Paulo, Brazil.

Adult moths of the *Phobetron* genus can resemble miniature frogs or even monkeys.

can detect the echolocation calls of these predators, producing involuntary neurological responses that cause the moth to fold its wings and fall directly to the ground.[16] Additionally, some species of tiger moths such as the Dogbane Tiger, *Cycnia tenera*, found in North America, produce ultrasonic sounds in response to the echolocation calls of bats to effectively jam or confuse their hunting strategies. There are even moths that adopt a form of Batesian acoustic mimicry for courtship as well as protection.[17] Colour may also play a role in evading nocturnal predators: it is possible that the high visibility of white or pale-coloured moths, which are easily spotted at dusk, is a type of protective warning colouration against bats.[18]

Other diurnal behavioural defence strategies include feigning death, the release of unpleasant chemicals, the emission of strange or unexpected sounds (in addition to anti-bat defences), erratic flight, 'flash colouration' from brightly coloured hindwings or the sudden display of eyespots to surprise potential predators such as

154

birds.[19] The Eyed Hawk-moth, *Smerinthus ocellatus*, for example, often rests on tree trunks by day with its 'bunched' wings resembling dry leaves; if disturbed, however, it flashes two bright blue eyespots on its pinkish hindwings in order to startle predators. The possession of eyespots is also used for 'body mirroring' so that an insect may appear to have two heads, thereby encouraging the predator to pounce on the false one. The presence of high levels of polymorphism, where one species has different forms, also serves as a defensive mechanism against the searching strategies of predators. The scarcity of a particular form can reduce levels of familiarity among predators, as can a high level of sympatric (same place) species diversity: in North America alone, for example, there are over 100 different red underwing species of the genus *Catocala* with often very subtle differences in their markings. 'Though birds learn when relationships are simple and systematic,' suggests the American entomologist Theodore Sargent, 'diversity makes for complex and unpredictable relationships which only confound the avian brain.'[20] If we add into the mix the short lifespans of many moths, then it becomes even harder for predators to remember their prey.

For most palatable species of moths that fly by night – unless they are Batesian mimics – the main survival strategy by day is to hide. To remain unseen, moths use a huge diversity of resting poses and wing patterns to produce a bewildering variety of cryptic defence strategies. The disguises adopted include wing patterns that resemble leaves, broken twigs or lichen-encrusted rocks. The patterns are often quite specific, such as the resemblance of the Miller Moth, *Acronicta leporina*, to the bark of birch trees on which it rests by day. Wing patterns may also include stripes or spots that break up the wing outline and make the moth harder to spot. In addition, unusual resting postures or strangely shaped wings can help the moth to blend into its

The Eyed Hawk moth, *Smerinthus ocellatus*, flashes its dramatic 'eyes' at would-be predators.

The Miller Moth, *Acronicta leporina*, rests by day on the bark of birch trees. This specimen was found in Spreewald, Brandenburg, Germany.

The spectacular *Antitrygodes divisaria* is found in South and East Asia. Its broken pattern might resemble dappled light within the forests where it is found.

surroundings. The moth *Tarsolepis sommeri* of the family Notodontidae, which is found in Borneo and other parts of the Malaysian Peninsula, has a wing pattern that resembles an empty space through which a broken twig protrudes (this moth is also known to be lachryphagous, or tear drinking, in its feeding habits since it has been observed drinking from around the eyes of forest animals such as tapirs). The curiously marked *Macrocilix maia*, a type of Drepanid moth found in China, Japan, Korea and elsewhere in East Asia, appears to have two flies on its wings that are feeding off bird excrement or some other kind of putrefied yellow liquid. And just in case this visual pattern fails to convince, the moth also emits a smell similar to bird droppings as an additional olfactory line of defence.

Moths not only seek out rocks, tree trunks or other surfaces but take care to position themselves carefully on them to make themselves as inconspicuous as possible, though whether the background

The lachryphagous (tear drinking) species of prominent moth, *Tarsolepis taiwana*, appears to include a void space in its wing pattern to radically break up its outline. This photograph is from Pu'er, Yunnan, China.

159

preferences of cryptic moths are actively 'chosen' rather than automatically adopted remains uncertain. This tendency to seek protection against different background colours or surfaces has been the source of some of the most remarkable research into what the British geneticist Michael Majerus termed 'evolution in action'.[21] A particular focus of interest has been the phenomenon of melanism – the prevalence of dark pigmentation – which occurs naturally but began to confer specific competitive advantages during the nineteenth century for many species occurring in soot-covered urban and industrial environments. The story of the Peppered Moth, *Biston betularia*, begins with the discovery in 1848, in a Manchester garden, of a black *carbonaria* form of what is normally a lightly speckled white moth. By the 1890s, nearly 90 per cent of the Peppered Moths in the Manchester area were black and, in 1896, the British entomologist James Tutt suggested the 'differential

The Drepanid moth *Macrocilix maia* has what appears to be two flies feeding off its wings. This moth was found in Fushan, Taiwan.

The rise of the melanic form of the Peppered Moth, *Biston betularia*, has been the focus of intense research and also controversy surrounding the effects of bird predation on evolution.

bird predation hypothesis' to account for this increase in the frequency of a previously rare form.[22] His basic thesis, investigated in field experiments by the British geneticist Bernard Kettlewell during the 1950s, was that the dark form had less chance of being spotted by birds when resting against soot-covered trees or buildings than the lightly speckled *typica* form. Further evidence for melanism in industrial areas was also provided by the increasing frequency of dark forms for many other species of moths found in urban and industrial areas of Europe and North America.[23]

More recently, however, these early studies of melanism have been criticized for methodological weaknesses, such as the deliberate placing of darker moths against pale surfaces to prove their vulnerability. It is now believed that this 'bird feeder' research design exaggerated the results, ignoring the ability of moths to seek appropriate substrates to hide against by day, even making small adjustments in their position in relation to bark striations or other patterned surfaces. Critics of Kettlewell's work note that little is known about how these species conceal themselves in natural situations since many Geometrid moths hide on the underside of leaves within tree canopies. Other concerns include the rise of melanism in *rural* areas of Europe and North America over the twentieth century, which cannot be explained by bird predation alone.

The scientific uncertainties over industrial melanism were heightened by the publication of Judith Hooper's book *Of Moths and Men: Intrigue, Tragedy, and the Peppered Moth* (2002), which alleged that Kettlewell's research had been not only flawed but fraudulent.[24] Creationists in the USA latched onto the controversy with glee and a leading biology textbook quietly dropped the Peppered Moth as an example of evolution.[25] In order to address this mounting scientific controversy, Michael Majerus undertook the original field experiments again over a seven-year period between 2001 and 2008 in order to address the weaknesses in Kettlewell's original research design. The study was carried out with a painstaking thoroughness and concern for eliminating the possibilities for bias introduced by placing moths in unnatural resting positions by day, and revealed that differential bird predation was indeed the critical factor in determining the relative dominance of pale and dark forms of the Peppered Moth, although the causal mechanisms are more complex than originally thought.[26] A further factor in the scientific mix is the fact that the Peppered Moth is strongly attracted to streetlights and other artificial sources of illumination, and will frequently settle on nearby surfaces such as walls where it is easily picked off by birds the next day.

A page of watercolours from the notebook of Joe Tilson in 1997 depicting various burnet moths (*Zygaena* spp.), which are among the most poisonous species of all.

B U R N E T S

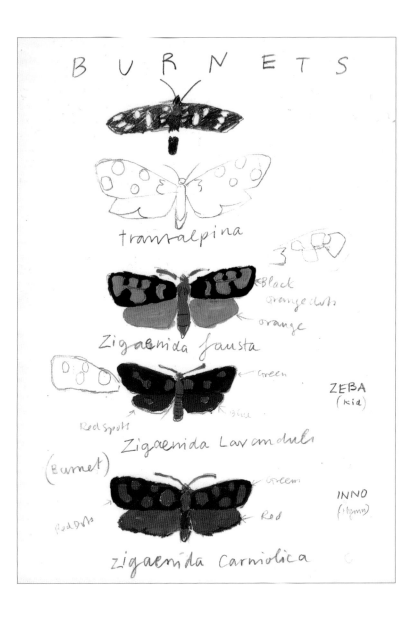

transalpina

3

Zigaemida fausta

←Black
orange dots
← orange

ZEBA
(kid)

← Green

← Blue

Red Spots

Zigaemida Lavandula

(Burnet)

Green

Red

INNO
(Hymn)

Red Dots

zigaemida Carniolica

In contrast to the melanic disguise of the Peppered Moth, there are many moths that seek protection in visibility, relying on their ability to use aposematic (warning) colouration to deter predators. These colour patterns are typically simple, consisting of brightly coloured bands, stripes or spots of two or three colours, which may also extend to the thorax or abdomen. The presence of Müllerian mimicry, whereby several, unpalatable forms adopt the same pattern or colouration, ensures that the colour combinations are straightforward and easily learnt by predators. Moths are able to use a wide variety of chemical compounds to produce toxins, either derived from the larval foodplant or synthesized in the body of the adult moth. The effect on predators varies from the merely distasteful to the highly toxic. For example, the brightly coloured burnet moths, of the family Zygaenidae, are among the most poisonous of all (they self-synthesize hydrogen cyanide). In contrast, various tiger moths from the subfamily Arctiinae use somewhat different chemical defences such as pyrrolizidine alkaloids and cardiac glycosides. In the case of the Garden Tiger, *Arctia caja*, some of the defence chemicals are derived from larval foodplants whereas others are self-synthesized by the adult moth. Research into Tiger Moths has also revealed that the caterpillars' consumption of pyrrolizidine alkaloids and iridoid glycosides produces specific morphogenetic effects, impacting on the development of the larvae, in an illustration of how these chemicals are woven into virtually every aspect of the insect's life cycle.[27]

By contrast, the palatable Batesian mimics adopt visual or even behavioural mimicry of other distasteful or dangerous organisms, including bees, wasps and other stinging insects. The various 'spider moths' found in rainforests appear to have multiple eyes and venomous fangs. The Lygodium Spider Moth, *Siamusotima aranea*, first described from northern Thailand in 2005, reveals leg-like markings across its wings when spread against a pale background. Some

species even elude spider predators not just by resembling them but also through adopting aspects of their behaviour: the *Brenthia* genus of metalmark moths confronts their jumping spider predators by pretending to be an aggressive adversary.[28] With Batesian mimicry, however, the number of palatable mimics must remain relatively low or the model itself is potentially placed in danger (which may partly explain the relative scarcity of some of these mimics). In practice, however, a spectrum of mimicry strategies between a 'pure' Batesian or Müllerian model can be observed with varying degrees of unpalatability and vulnerability (that may also be affected by the degree of hunger experienced by predators).[29]

Historically, the degree of perfection displayed by some mimics has provoked uncertainty over the limits to Darwinian evolution.

The Garden Tiger, *Arctia caja*, with its bright aposematic (warning) colours, sequesters plant toxins and also manufactures its own additional toxins.

The Clearwing Moth, *Negotinthia myrmosaeformis*, from the family Sesiidae is a hymenopteroid mimic complete with yellow tufts on its legs that resemble pollen baskets. This specimen was found in Chaskowo, Bulgaria.

Among the most influential critics of the reductionist aspects to evolutionary theory is the novelist Vladimir Nabokov, who suggested that there must be something more than mere natural selection involved given the exquisite degree of refinement of many insect mimics. In his autobiography, *Speak, Memory*, for example, Nabokov reflects on a caterpillar that is shaped like a larva caught in the jaws of an ant:

> Consider the tricks of an acrobatic caterpillar (of the Lobster moth) which in infancy looks like bird's dung, but after molting develops scrabbly hymenopteroid appendages and baroque characteristics, allowing the extraordinary fellow

to play two parts at once (like the actor in Oriental shows that *becomes* a pair of intertwisted wrestlers): that of a writhing larva and that of a big ant seemingly harrowing it.[30]

Nabokov continues, marvelling at the excess of detail in nature:

When a certain moth resembles a certain wasp in shape and colour, it also walks and moves its antennae in a waspish, unmoth like manner. When a butterfly has to look like a leaf, not only are all the details of a leaf beautifully rendered but markings mimicking grub-bored holes are generously thrown in. 'Natural selection,' in the Darwinian sense could not explain the miraculous coincidence of imitative aspect

The caterpillar of the Lobster Moth, *Stauropus fagi*, inspired Vladimir Nabokov's doubts over the degree of refinement achievable under Darwinian evolution.

and imitative behaviour, nor could one appeal to 'the struggle of life' when a protective device was carried to a point of mimetic subtlety, exuberance, and luxury far in excess of a predator's power of appreciation. I discovered in nature the nonutilitarian delights that I sought in art. Both were a form of magic, both were a game of intricate enchantment and deception.[31]

These reflections, along with some brief passages from *The Gift* (1963), are all that remains of Nabokov's lost essay on the limits to Darwinian theory.[32] But what are we to make of Nabokov's claim that natural selection cannot account for the refinement of mimicry in the natural world? Nabokov was no creationist, but he did incline towards vitalism, searching (like Bergson) for some kind of life force beyond the mere mechanics of what he understood to be population genetics. Although defenders of Nabokov have tried to place him in the vanguard of post-Darwinian approaches to evolution, his perspectives on mimicry lie closer to a transitional phase in late nineteenth-century scientific thought when the apparent simplicity of Darwinism was still being widely contested. Nabokov's own research, undertaken at Harvard's Museum of Comparative Zoology in the 1940s, remains a respected contribution to taxonomy (especially in relation to Lycaenid butterflies, known as 'the blues'), but it seems that he never developed a sophisticated grasp of population genetics or articulated an alternative theory of evolution that could have gained wider scientific credence.[33]

There are, however, parallels between Nabokov's focus on the 'nonutilitarian delights' of insect mimicry and the surrealist writer Roger Caillois' anti-Darwinian stance developed in his essay 'Mimicry and Legendary Psychasthenia', first published in 1935.[34]Among Caillois' examples are the leaf- or petal-mimicking mantises, the Eyed Hawk-moth (*Smerinthus ocellatus*), and also various Geometrid caterpillars that resemble thorns. Like Nabokov, Caillois finds that 'imitation is pushed to the smallest details', and he draws on a striking passage from Rémy Perrier's *Cours élémentaire de zoologie*, first published in 1899, to illustrate his point:

the wings bear gray-green spots simulating the mold of lichens and glistening surfaces that give them the look of torn and perforated leaves: 'including spots of mold of the sphaeriaceous kind that stud the leaves of these plants; everything, including the transparent scars produced by phytophagic insects when, devouring the parenchyma of the leaves in places, they leave only the translucid skin.

The bird dropping mimic *Eudryas grata* is found in North America.

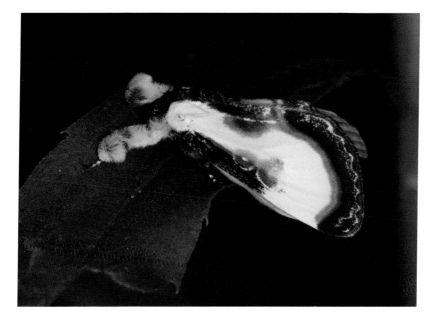

The superb dead leaf mimic *Uropyia meticulodina* photographed in Taiwan.

Imitations are produced by pearly spots that correspond to similar spots on the upper surface of the wings.'[35]

For Caillois, these forms of mimetic adaptation go far beyond chance, as intimated by the French biologist Lucien Cuénot.[36] Caillois draws on a modified Lamarckian theory of inherited traits to suggest the existence of 'environmental mirroring', whereby an organism reproduces its environment in its body in a manner that is considered analogous to a kind of three-dimensional photography:

> Morphological mimicry could then be, after the fashion of chromatic mimicry, an actual photography, but of the form and the relief, a photography on the level of the object and not on that of the image, a reproduction in three-dimensional space with solids and voids: sculpture-photography or better

teleplasty, if one strips the word of any metapsychical content.[37]

However, far from seeing this as an effective adaptation, Caillois does not accept that visual mimicry can be a dependable form of defence since it only works against predators that rely on sight rather than smell (we now know this is incorrect, since various forms of olfactory mimicry do exist). This leads him to conclude, with Cuénot, that the 'epiphenomenon' of mimicry is of little practical utility to an organism and may even create new dangers:

> We are thus dealing with a luxury and even a dangerous luxury, for there are cases in which mimicry causes the creature to go from bad to worse: geometer-moth caterpillars simulate shoots of shrubbery so well that gardeners cut them with their pruning shears.[38]

Instead, Caillois suggests that imitation is a kind of biomorphic relic from a more primitive state of nature. He interprets mimicry as a form of residual magic left over from an earlier evolutionary phase when organisms possessed a greater degree of 'plasticity'. For Caillois, the phenomenon of mimicry in insects 'would thus be accurately defined as *an incantation fixed at its culminating point* and having caught the sorcerer in his own trap'.[39] This invocation of 'magic' in nature has affinities with Nabokov's search for an explanation that lies beyond the utilitarian realm of population genetics. Yet many of these concerns with the meaning of mimicry do not ultimately stem from scientific disputes over evolution but rather from a cultural ambivalence towards the aesthetic characteristics of modernity.

More recently there has been scientific recognition of the limitations to more simplistic accounts of evolution. Greater emphasis has been placed on the detailed timescales and mechanisms involved in the development of mimicry and polymorphism.[40] In terms of mimicry, a two-step evolutionary process is now widely acknowledged in which a random major mutation that confers some degree of advantage in Batesian or Müllerian terms is subsequently refined by further minor mutations to produce some of the spectacular examples found in nature.

8 Spinners and Monsters

Patience is power: with time and patience the mulberry
becomes silk.
Japanese proverb[1]

The most direct role that moths have played in human history is
through the production of silk. The caterpillar of the silk moth –
better known as the silkworm – produces a commodity that is
unrivalled in its aesthetic allure and practical versatility. As one of
the earliest luxury commodities, silk was indispensible for the
development of early trade networks and has even served as a form
of currency. Silk is a hybrid entity par excellence – an organic fabric
that is nevertheless derived from elements of both biological and
cultural evolution.

Only honey can rival silk as the most important commodity
produced by insects for human consumption, yet the cultural and
symbolic associations are very different. In his beekeeping manual
The Feminist Monarchie, first published in 1609, Charles Butler
reflects on the moral superiority of beekeeping compared with the
recent arrival of silk production in early modern England:

> For the fruite of the Silkeworme serveth only to cover the
> bodie; but the fruite of the Bee to nourish and cure it: that is
> to bee applied outwardly, this to be invvardly received: that
> for comlinesse and conveniency, this for health & necessitie.[2]

Silk has always held an ambiguous association with human culture
since it is not a necessity, and it does not 'nourish' the body as

Butler attests, and yet it has nonetheless played such a significant role in human history. In terms of its fineness, strength and thermal properties, silk surpasses the qualities of any other known fibres, whether natural or synthetic.[3]

The biological origins of silk lie in specialized salivary glands of caterpillars that are connected to an organ called the spinneret. The main biological function of silk is to create a tough cocoon that can shield the vulnerable pupa from predators. Silk is also used for other forms of protection: it can enable caterpillars to pull leaves together to form a protective shelter; it can be used to attach small pieces of leaves or other organic detritus as a form of camouflage; and a single thread of silk can allow caterpillars to 'abseil' from danger without losing their spot.

In the case of the domesticated silk moth, *Bombyx mori*, the cocoon is derived from one unbroken thread of silk up to 1,200 m (4,000 ft) long, and this silk forms the basis of sericulture (the farming of silk). This silk strand is composed of two sets of proteins – fibroin and sericin – which produce a complex crystalline structure with a range of unique properties.[4] Before hatching, however, the silkworms are killed (usually by steaming) to prevent the thread from being broken.

Most silk is produced by a single species of silk moth, *Bombyx mori*, and its domestication began in China nearly 7,000 years ago. In evolutionary terms, it is probably a descendent of *Bombyx mandarina*, which is still found in China, Korea and Japan today. Unlike its ancestors, however, the domesticated silk moth no longer flies and the caterpillars, or 'worms', rarely wander from their only foodplant, the mulberry tree. Of the various types of mulberry tree it is the White Mulberry, *Morus alba*, originating in northern China, that is by far the most important food source for *Bombyx mori*, and the tree has been extensively cultivated all over the world in order to support silk production.

Early 20th-century German poster showing the four main species of moths used for silk production: *Bombyx mori*, *Hyalophora cecropia*, *Antheraea pernyi* and *Samia cynthia*.

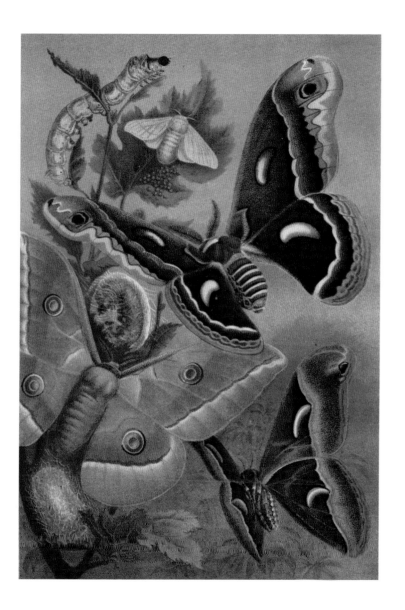

In addition to *Bombyx mori* there are three further types of silk that are of commercial significance: eri, muga and tussah. Eri silk is derived from the Ailanthus Silk Moth, *Samia cynthia*, originating from China and Korea, and its production process differs from that of silk produced by *Bombyx mori* because the moth leaves the cocoon before it is spun. Since the larvae are not destroyed in the production process, eri silk is sometimes referred to as the 'fabric of peace' and is preferred by religious denominations who do not wish to kill insects. However, eri silk is not so versatile or easily woven, and has consequently been used on a much smaller scale. Other wild varieties of silk, also cultivated in India, include muga silk produced by the Assam Silk moth, *Antheraea assamensis*, and tussah silk produced the Tussah Silk moth, *Antheraea mylitta*.

Fabric design with eri silk, known as the 'fabric of peace' since the silkworms are not killed after they spin their cocoons.

There are several other types of silk moth that have also been harvested for 'wild silk' at various points in human history. Before the arrival of *Bombyx mori* in Europe, for example, other species of moth were used for the production of a poorer quality silk than that originating in China. From about 700 BCE there is evidence of sericulture on the Dodecanese island of Kos, using the European silk moth, *Pachypasa otus*, which produced a kind of silk referred to by the Romans as *bombycinae vestes*. As early as the fifth century BCE, however, fragments of Chinese silk have been found in Greece, suggesting that some international trade in this precious fabric was already underway.[5]

Silk was produced at a very early stage in Chinese civilization. There is archaeological evidence for silk dating back to the Neolithic Hemudu and Liangzhu cultures in eastern China, and for silk-weaving dating back to 3630 BCE, although earlier artefacts such as an ivory bowl with possible silkworm decorations, dating from around 4900 BCE, have also been recovered. The scale of sericulture in China certainly increased from around 2600 BCE, and especially under the Eastern Zhou Dynasty (771–221 BCE), with silk used not only for clothes but flags, tents, paper, strings for musical instruments and other products. The production methods remained a closely guarded secret for millennia, although there is a possibility that silkworm eggs were smuggled in the fifth century CE to the trading post of Hetian (now located in the Chinese province of Xinjiang).[6] Elsewhere in East Asia, sericulture reached Korea around 200 BCE, and then Japan at about 300 CE (at the end of the Yayoi period), followed by India and Persia (now Iran) at about 400 CE.[7]

As trading routes between China and Europe opened up during the Han Dynasty (206 BCE–220 CE), silk proved to be an extremely precious commodity: by the time it reached the Roman Empire it was reputedly worth its weight in gold. Under Augustus (27 BCE–14 CE), the first Roman emperor, the silk trade increased significantly,

Detail of painting depicting silk production in China, early 12th century, by Emperor Huizong of Song, after a now-lost 8th-century original by Zhang Xuan.

in part due to greater political stability, more regularized trading arrangements and territorial consolidation, which reduced the level of risk experienced by merchants over the immense distances that commodities had to be transported.[8] Silk rapidly gained notoriety because of its great expense: in the first century BCE silk was so rare in Rome that even the richest citizens could only afford strips of silk that were attached to their clothes, yet even these small pieces of fabric denoted higher social status or political power. Over time, however, the popularity of Chinese silk provoked anxiety because of the way it drained wealth away from the Roman economy. Pliny, for example, bemoaned the loss of the Empire's wealth to pay for luxuries, which included not only silk but emeralds and pearls. Such was the demand for silk that in 14 CE the Roman senate outlawed the wearing of silk by men in an unsuccessful attempt to limit its popularity, and the emperor Aurelian (r. 270–75 CE) forbade even his own household from wearing it.[9]

The term 'silk road' or rather 'silk routes' (*Seidenstraßen*) was first coined by the Austrian geographer Ferdinand von Richthofen in 1877, and refers to a network of trade routes for silk and other commodities such as salt, wool and jade, which ran west from what is now Xi'an, the former Han capital city.[10] Traces of silk have been found in graves dating from around 1500 BCE in the region of Bactria (now lying between Afghanistan and Tajikistan), but it is uncertain whether this fabric originated from China or was locally produced. In the second century CE sericulture became established in the vast Sassanid empire of Persia (224–651 CE), a result of military conflict which was itself partly driven by attempts to control the silk trade.[11] By the eighth century CE silk was also being produced in Sogdiana (now part of present-day Tajikistan and Uzbekistan), and the skills of Chinese prisoners of war were used for the development of Arab silk-weaving in Damascus.[12]

So dominant was silk in these trading routes that it became a form of currency. Under Emperor Xuanzong (712–56 CE) of the Tang Dynasty, the Chinese military became increasingly reliant on Uighur supplies of cavalry horses, each of which was exchanged for between 40 and 50 bolts of silk (one bolt consisted of about 9 metres of cloth, which was equivalent to the maximum amount that one skilled weaver could produce during a day's work). While silk had already been used extensively in the collection of tax revenues in China under the Han Dynasty, over time it was adopted as a form of international currency.[13]

Silk production reached Europe during the Byzantine era as its capital, Constantinople (now Istanbul), emerged as the largest and most prosperous city in the world. An apocryphal account suggests that in the year 552 Emperor Justinian used monks to smuggle the eggs of *Bombyx mori* from China to Constantinople in an early example of industrial espionage, although this is now disputed since sericulture was already practised in sixth-century Syria, which was then part of the Byzantine empire.[14] In the seventh century CE the spread of Arab influence in Europe and North Africa brought sericulture and silk-weaving to Morocco, Spain, Sicily and southern Italy, and by the tenth century the Spanish region of Andalusia had become the centre of a European silk industry. Silk-making artisans themselves travelled widely across Europe since their skills were in such demand. By the twelfth century sericulture was established across most of Italy, including northern city-states such as Genoa and Lucca. European silk-making was also facilitated by technical improvements, especially in Italy, such as Leonardo da Vinci's invention of a new type of spindle that could work on three threads simultaneously. The production of higher quality threads also enabled the production of new fabrics such as satins, velvets and the inclusion of metal threads of silver and gold to produce sumptuous visual effects.[15]

In 1536 King François I of France granted Lyon a monopoly of the European silk trade, but after the Revocation of the Edict of Nantes by King Louis XIV in 1685, and the intensified persecution of Huguenots, there was a dispersal of silk-making skills across Europe, and especially to England under the Protestant monarch James I.[16] London's Spitalfields, for example, emerged as a major centre for Huguenot silk-weaving, as skilled French and Flemish refugees arrived there fleeing from religious persecution.

The rise of the English silk industry in the early seventeenth century was driven by growing demand in the late Elizabethan period for luxury commodities such as silk stockings (manufactured from around 1560 onwards) and political anxieties over the country's reliance on imported products from France, Italy and Spain (although Italy retained an almost complete monopoly on raw or semi-finished threads).[17] The increasing popularity of silk in early seventeenth-century England was evidently a source of mirth: in Shakespeare's *King Lear*, for example, Oswald, the

Illustration of silk-weaving from Giovanni Boccaccio, *De claris mulieribus* (c. 1374).

Johannes Stradanus, *Feeding the Silkworms* I, c. 1590. A Flemish artist active in Italy, where this series of engravings may have been made.

Johannes Stradanus, *Women Winding Silk*, c. 1590.

Johannes Stradanus, *Feeding the Silkworms* II, c. 1580.

Johannes Stradanus, *Preparing the Eggs of Silkworms*, c. 1590.

steward of King Lear's daughter Goneril, is subjected to a tirade of sartorial insults by the Earl of Kent, who calls him, among other things, 'three suited' (possibly referring to his frippery and pretensions to a higher social station) and also a 'filthy, worsted-stocking knave' (a pointed reference to one who wears wool rather than silk).

It was widely anticipated that the promotion of sericulture in England would not only enrich individual producers but create employment. Yet a moral and political ambiguity permeates the early modern discussion of sericulture in seventeenth-century England, since silk held such a close association with indolence, luxury and emerging forms of conspicuous consumption, which seemed to be an individual pleasure rather than a collective good. Whereas bees have tended to be anthropomorphized as diligent, dutiful and well-organized workers, silkworms were often portrayed as the organic analogue of the pampered and wealthy elite for whom the silk they produce is intended. The worms have been characterized as fussy or sensitive to unwanted noise or smells, with their human contact best restricted to only certain types of people.[18] The newly appointed Keeper of the King's Silkworms, William Stallenge, for example, required that the silk farm or 'magnanerie' (from the French patois *magnan*) must smell sweet with sprinklings of herbs such as lavender and thyme.[19] Similarly, writing in 1766, Moses Harris remarks of silkworms:

> They are naturally tender, and subject to several Diseases, to prevent which, those, whose business it is to keep them for sake of their Silk, keep them very clean and dry, often removing them for Change of air, perfuming the Room wherein they are fed with Incense; they likewise suffer by Thunder, Firing of Guns or any harsh Sound . . .[20]

THE
Silkewormes, and
their Flies:

Liuely deſcribed in verſe, by T. M.
a *Countrie Farmar*, and an ap-
prentice in Phyſicke.

For the great benefit and enriching of England.

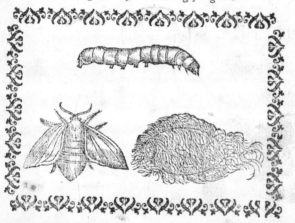

Printed at London by V. S. for Nicholas Ling, and
are to be ſold at his ſhop at the Weſt ende of
Paules. 1 5 9 9.

Thomas Moffet,
*The Silkewormes
and their Flies*
(1599).

There were counter-arguments to these ideas: Thomas Moffet penned a didactic poem *The Silkewormes and their Flies* (1599) praising the chastity and diligence of silkworms – although of course the larvae cannot breed – arguing that because they 'onely keepe themsleues to one' they should be placed in the morally upstanding entomological universe of worker bees. In other respects, however, he acknowledges that the silkworms are pampered – not least through the need to plant many thousands of mulberry trees to provide their only accepted source of food.[21] Moffet's encomium to silkworms forms part of an ironic genre of late sixteenth-century poetry that is suffused with a mix of pastoral imagery and wry humour.[22]

Behind these sixteenth- and seventeenth-century ambivalences in the depiction of the silkworm were a new set of ideas about the relationship of private consumption to public virtue. Did spending on luxury goods benefit the common good, or was it a selfish act that weakened the nation and encouraged feckless behaviour? The production of silk, with its attendant forms of labour alienation and commodity fetishism, marked a significant element in the nascent transition to a fully fledged capitalist society, and the silkworm holds a special position in these discourses because it was seen as providing a kind of 'free', non-human labour for the benefit of human societies. This is explicitly referred to by Moffet, who praises silk as 'Quintessence, / Made without hands byond al humane sense'.[23] Yet the perception of a commodity produced without work was disturbed by the very real division of human labour that was involved: whereas apiculture manuals were aimed at beekeepers, as both hive-owners and specialized workers, the promotion of sericulture required more stratified forms of labour with oversight undertaken by a 'mulberry elite' of entrepreneurial industrialists.[24] While one set of writers could argue that silk was produced without labour, another saw it as the model for the way in which work could

Portrait entitled *A Lady of Rank* from the Parham House collection, Sussex. Note how the silk dress has silkworm designs on the sleeves.

instil a greater degree of social order. The Italian alchemist and physician Leonardo Fioravanti (1518–1588), for example, described how 'silk has its own court of law that administers justice without anyone who interferes'.[25] The magic of sericulture for Fioravanti seemed to extend to a kind of natural law that mirrored existing social distinctions along with prevailing conceptions of justice and obligation.

However, while contemporary guides to sericulture might stress the moral and disciplining effects of silk production, there were also very visible signs of human involvement in the trade. Silk-weaving was a gruelling and highly mechanized profession well before the Industrial Revolution. In W. G. Sebald's words, many workers 'spent their lives with their wretched bodies strapped to looms made of wooden frames and rails, hung with weights, and reminiscent of instruments of torture or cages'.[26] It was even altering the way that cities looked and felt and the rhythms of traditional life: Sebald describes the blaze of light emanating from weavers' workshops, used to extend the working day beyond nightfall.

There were also early attempts to export sericulture to England's colonies. The Anglo-German polymath Samuel Hartlib, in his *Legacy of Husbandry* (1651), suggested that the plentiful supplies of labour should be put to work, not simply to raise private profit, but also to contribute towards the 'Publique Good', calling for it to be extended to newly acquired overseas colonies.[27] Yet English attempts to introduce plantation sericulture to Virginia and South Carolina in the early seventeenth century failed, just as Spanish attempts had in Hispaniola a century earlier. These early endeavours to transplant the 'natural wealth' of mulberry trees between different geographical contexts anticipate the interest of colonial botany in coaxing 'exotic' plants to flourish in the cool and misty landscapes of seventeenth-century England as well as the extension of plantation agriculture in the New World.[28]

In practice, however, the complexities of silk production, including the cultivation of mulberry trees, proved to consist of a far more intricate process than that of beekeeping. The seventeenth-century craze for sericulture in early modern England turned out to be a failure, establishing only a small domestic silk industry (although this has persisted into the modern era, as its small-scale, high-quality production make it ideal for highly exclusive commissions such as royal weddings or coronations). Simultaneously, the European silk industry fell into steep decline as a result of competition from other fibres such as cotton, and later viscose, along with the destructive impact of diseases affecting both silkworms and mulberry trees. Even innovations such as the Jacquard loom in 1801, a forerunner of the analytical engine of Charles Babbage and the modern computer, could not save European production.[29]

By the late nineteenth century, global patterns of sericulture had significantly changed, with Japan surpassing China as the main producer of raw silk. Under the accelerated modernization of Japan under the Meiji Restoration (1868–1912), silk emerged as one of the country's major export industries, bolstered by technological improvements in reeling and other aspects of production.[30] With the completion of the Suez Canal in 1869, Japanese imports of raw silk also became more competitively priced in Europe despite efforts to industrialize production in France and elsewhere. By the late 1930s, Japan was producing three-quarters of the world's raw silk, and (with the exception of the wartime interregnum, which emboldened failed attempts to rekindle European self-sufficiency) it remained the main global source until 1970, when China regained its former dominance.

Although the economic significance of silk for Japan had begun to wane by the early 1960s, the silkworm made a dramatic comeback in the form of the cultural icon 'Mothra'. The name for this *kaiju* (the Japanese word for 'monstrous beast') is derived from the words 'moth' and 'mother', and Mothra is a combination of the domesticated silkworm or Kaiko (蚕) with other wild species such as the Yamamayu (Japanese oak silkmoth), *Antheraea yamamai*; the Kususan (Japanese giant silk worm), *Caligula japonica*; and one of the largest moths in the world, the Yonagunisan (Atlas Moth), *Attacus atlas ryukyuensis*.[31] While other giant monsters such as Godzilla or Radon used the exotic and temporally remote figure of the dinosaur as their prototype, Mothra was conceived as a 'domestically produced monster' that was nonetheless capable of springing a surprise attack on the U.S. and other perceived enemies: tellingly, Mothra emerged in the context of a campaign against the Japan–U.S. Security Treaty of 1960. The first Mothra film was released in 1961, at a point when silk was still a very significant component of the Japanese economy, and is loosely based on the serialized novel *The Luminous Fairies and Mothra,* by Takehiko Fukunaga, Shinichiro

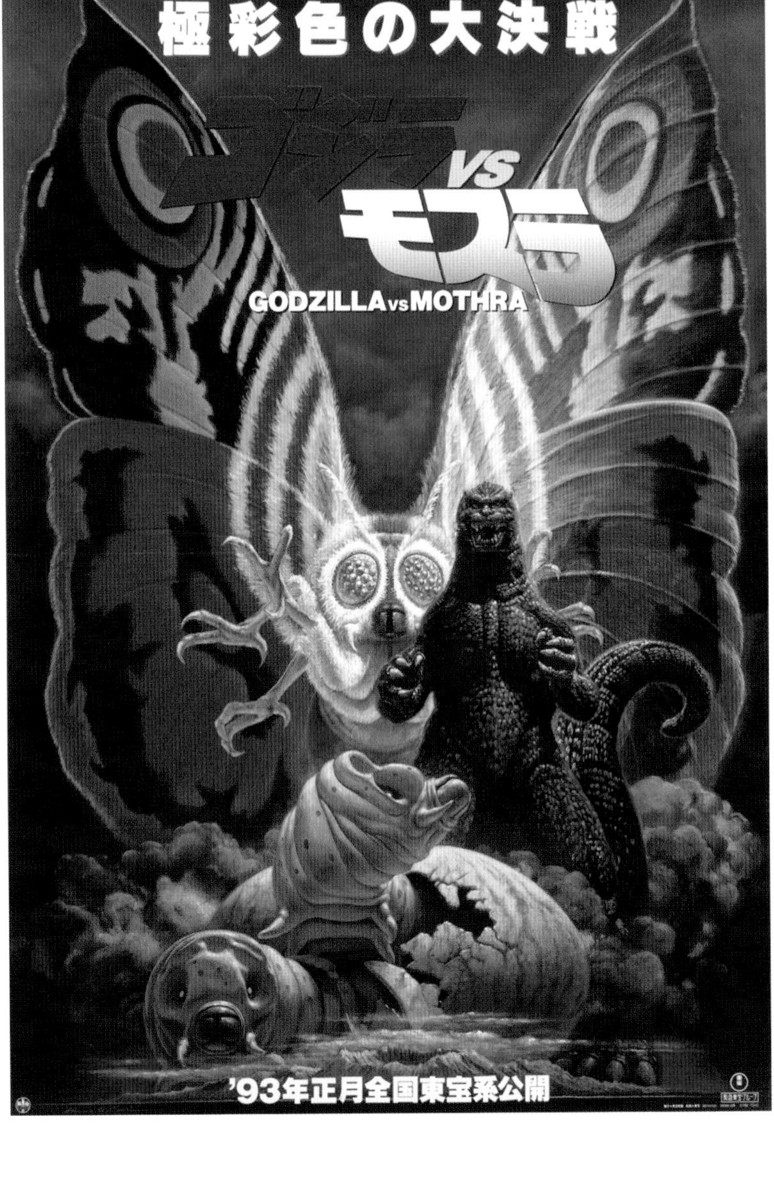
極彩色の大決戦
ゴジラ VS モスラ
GODZILLA VS MOTHRA
'93年正月全国東宝系公開

Nakamura and Yoshie Hotta, which appeared in the sensationalist *Asahi Weekly* magazine in the late 1950s.[32]

In the original story Mothra hatches from a giant egg washed up on the fictitious Infant Island, which is depicted as a site of former nuclear testing, located in the Polynesian South Seas, now reimagined as a magical zone 'shrouded in exotic yet nostalgic ambience'.[33] The figure of Mothra thus enabled a kind of romantic escapism, obscuring Japan's own colonial history in the subtropical belt to the south of its islands, and articulated an imagined sense of cultural and historical continuity during a period of social and economic upheaval. The associations with silk meant that Mothra could also be conceived as a kind of cultural nostalgia for a mythical 'Silk Land' where 'silkmoths swarmed over mulberry leaves in the dusk and wild oak moths silently spread their wings in the forests'.[34] There are also cultural continuities with pre-industrial silk deities such as the goddess Oshira-sama, worshipped in many agricultural regions of Japan. In contrast to other monsters in Japanese popular culture such as Godzilla, Mothra's monstrosity does not embody

Mothra clearly has the advantage, in *Mothra vs. Godzilla* (1964).

191

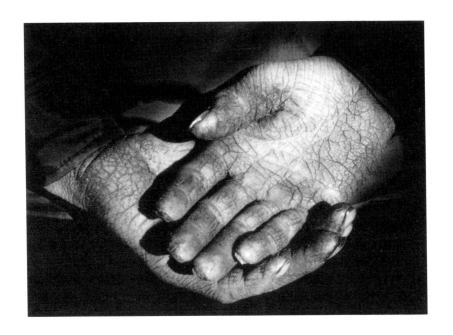

Minami Yoshikazu, *21 sai no yome no te* (Hands of the 21-year-old bride), photograph, 1963.

Liang Shaoji, *Chains/the Unbearable Lightness of Being/Nature Series no. 79* (2003–7).

Liang Shaoji, *Bed/Nature Series no. 10* (1993–9).

the threat of nuclear weapons and their use in Hiroshima and Nagasaki: rather, Mothra is a protective and comforting monster.

By the final film, *Mothra vs. Godzilla* (1964), Mothra had become a completely benign protector, a kind of 'modern day silk deity', as film-makers sought to downplay the rising tensions in Japanese society that would explode in extensive street protests by the late 1960s.[35] However, the nostalgia associated with Mothra obscured the harsh realities of silk production in Japan during this period. These are captured symbolically in Minami Yoshikazu's 1963 photograph of the cracked hands of a young female worker operating under the agrarian patriarchy of Japanese sericulture.[36] The picture points to the unsung and largely invisible place of cheap and 'dexterous' female labour in achieving the Japanese 'economic miracle'

192

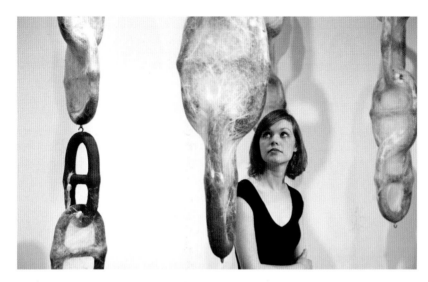

(the shift away from the export of agricultural products such as raw silk towards the global sale of electronic goods), revealing the economic monstrosity of capitalist sericulture and its 'invisible labour' in the modern age.

Silk has made a poignant reappearance in Chinese culture through the art installations of Liang Shaoji, who has been using silkworms extensively since the late 1980s. In a series of recent works Shaoji has played on the similarity in sound between the Chinese words for 'silkworm', 'dilapidation' and 'meditation' to explore the meaning of nature in contemporary culture.[37] In installations such as *Chains/The Unbearable Lightness of Being/Nature series no. 79* (2003–7) and *Whirl* (2012) he allows objects such as cobblestones or metal chains to become gradually enveloped in silk as part of a strange transformation. In *Listening to the Silkworm/Nature series no. 98* (2006–9) an auditory dimension is added through the amplified sound of live silkworms eating mulberry leaves. These living sculptures bring gallery spaces into the mysterious realm of sericulture and its dependence on many thousands of living organisms.

Silk, once the realm of extravagance, has now become an almost ubiquitous commodity: high-street chains offer mass-produced silk shirts for a fraction of the price once associated with luxury clothing. Yet the complexities and oddities of silk production still engender a sense of the uncanny in relation to the cruelty of the fate awaiting the industrious silkworms and the hidden human labour behind the production of fine clothes.

9 Lines of Flight

A good night for mothing
Vladimir Nabokov

When Nabokov submitted the final manuscript of his novel *Bend Sinister*, his editor queried if the final word of the last sentence should read 'nothing' rather than 'mothing'. By 'mothing' Nabokov had a very particular activity in mind: the nocturnal adventure of finding moths; and it was on just such a night – close, still and moonless – that he had found his new species of pug clinging to a motel window in Utah.

There is a world of difference between the vivid appearance of living moths and the often faded specimens to be found in museums or photographic plates. An encounter with the multitude of moths swirling around a light, or more dramatically still, a purpose-built moth trap with a white sheet for observation, is a truly extraordinary experience: moths constitute part of the entomological sublime derived from their bewildering diversity of forms, patterns and colours. Even in more remote temperate zones, let alone global biodiversity hotspots, new species are constantly turning up as part of the fabulous realm of the taxonomic unknown.

The more bizarre forms of mimicry and disguise have even contributed towards lingering uncertainties over the origins and purpose of biological diversity. Yet the recurring fascination with vitalism or some other kind of 'life force' is best conceived as a form of scientific romanticism: a hope that there might still be traces of magic or mystery that lie beyond reductionist forms of scientific explanation. Although doubts over the sophistication of evolution have been repeatedly dispelled, the precise mechanisms by which a caterpillar or adult moth comes to resemble something other than itself remain a source of wonder.

The moth is as much a cultural phenomenon as a scientific fact. Moths have been integral to the rise of natural history as a distinctive phase in the history of knowledge, replacing mythological schemas with emphasis on direct observation, and gradually extending towards the inner workings of insect bodies and their evolutionary relationships. Yet modern taxonomy is now in the throes of a 'double crisis' driven by a lack of resources to study life on earth and its accelerated rate of destruction. The status of taxonomy since the nineteenth century has waned with the gradual divergence of natural history from the natural sciences and the declining status of field observation in comparison with better funded laboratory-based research. Although DNA barcoding presents a certain kind of technical fix to the lack of time to inventory insect biodiversity, as we saw in the opening chapter, its wider implications for phylogenetic research or conservation biology remain uncertain.

The world of moths is now the focus of renewed interest facilitated by advances in digital photography and the sharing of scientific expertise. The Internet has provided new possibilities for the rapid sharing of scientific knowledge that might once have been held in only a handful of libraries, museums or universities: it is now possible to identify many moths in a matter of minutes by consulting specialist websites or connecting with virtual communities of enthusiasts and experts. There are also increasing numbers of events that enable wider participation in scientific research, such as 'moth nights' and other activities in Europe, in North America and increasingly in East Asia, that serve to further public understanding of biodiversity through direct contact with living insects. The UK Parliament even has an unofficial parliamentary spokesperson for moths, Madeleine Moon MP, and a moth trap is occasionally run from the roof of the House of Commons.

Moths seem to flit between the arts and the sciences, whether in terms of their names, cultural symbolism or attempts to understand their perceptual realm. Although the figure of the moth has most often served as a metaphor for death, darkness or erotic infatuation, its cultural and material presence extends far beyond these familiar tropes to include the pollination of flowers and even the clothes we wear.

Timeline of the Moth

146–100 MYA	100–90 MYA	60–50 MYA	4,900 BCE
First definitive Lepidoptera fossils found in amber (oldest from the Mesozoic/Lower Cretaceous period)	Fossil leaf mines found in Mid-Cretaceous Dakota Formation. Rapid co-evolution of Lepidoptera with the rise of angiosperms (flowering plants)	Co-evolution of moths and bats during the Early Tertiary era	Neolithic cultures in what is now eastern China begin silk production

1705	1734–42	1758	1763
Maria Sibylla Merian publishes *Metamorphosis insectorum surinamensium*	René-Antoine Ferchault de Réaumur publishes *Mémoires pour servir à l'histoire des insectes*	Carl Linnaeus introduces the modern binomial system of nomenclature for Lepidoptera in his *Systema naturae*	Giovanni Antonio Scopoli publishes *Entomologia carniolica*

1878	1896	1950S
Fritz Müller proposes the concept of Müllerian mimicry, based on poisonous organisms sharing similar types of colours or patterns	James Tutt suggests that the rise of melanism in moths in industrial Manchester might be caused by differential bird predation	Growing use of Robinson-type moth traps expands the scope and effectiveness of fieldwork including long-term sampling of population change

| 77–79 CE | 1602 | 1634 | 1669 |

Pliny the Elder describes several species of moths in his *Natural History*

Ulisse Aldrovandi publishes *De animalibus insectis*

Posthumous publication of *Theatrum insectorum* by Thomas Moffet and other scholars

Jan Swammerdam publishes *Historia insectorum generalis*

| 1766 | 1775 | 1848–59 |

Moses Harris publishes *The Aurelian or Natural History of English Insects: Namely, Moths and Butterflies. Together with the plants on which they feed*

Michael Denis and Ignaz Schiffermüller publish *Ankündung eines systematischen Werkes von den Schmetterlingen der Wienergegend*

Henry Walter Bates observes insect mimicry in Amazonia, after which 'Batesian mimicry' is termed. Bates's work is a major influence on Charles Darwin

| 1980s | 1990s | 2000s |

Daniel Janzen and his colleagues develop parataxonomy in Costa Rica in order to rapidly expand knowledge of biodiversity

The use of DNA barcoding reveals the presence of many cryptic species, challenging existing approaches to taxonomy

Various studies show significant declines in moth abundance that may parallel bee decline

References

1 MULTITUDES

1　Carl Linnaeus, *Systema naturae: per regna tria naturæ, secundum classes, ordines, genera, species, cum characteribus, differentiis, synonymis, locis* (Holmiæ [Stockholm], 1758), English trans. cited in A. Maitland Emmet, *The Scientific Names of the British Lepidoptera* (Colchester, 1991), p. 16.

2　W. G. Sebald, *Austerlitz*, trans. Anthea Bell [2001] (London, 2002), p. 127.

3　Carl Linnaeus, *Systema naturae, sive regna tria naturæ systematice proposita per classes, ordines, genera, et species* (Lugduni Batavorum [Leiden], 1735).

4　William Shakespeare, cited in Kjell B. Sandved and Jo Brewer, *Butterflies* (New York, 1976), p. 74.

5　See Niels P. Kristensen, Malcolm J. Scoble and Ole Karsholt, 'Lepidoptera Phylogeny and Systematics: The State of Inventorying Moth and Butterfly Diversity', *Zootaxa*, MDCLXVIII (2007), pp. 699–747.

6　In terms of evolutionary proximity the most closely related insect order to the Lepidoptera is the Trichoptera (the caddis-flies, or 'sedge flies'), of which around 12,000 species have been described.

7　Edward O. Wilson, *The Diversity of Life* [1992] (London, 2001), p. xii.

8　See Pierre André Latreille, *Précis des caractères génériques des insectes, disposés dans un ordre naturel* (Bordeaux, 1796).

9 See Jean Baptiste Boisduval, *Histoire naturelle des insectes: species général des Lépidoptères* (Paris, 1836).

10 Moses Harris, *The Aurelian or Natural History of English Insects: Namely, Moths and Butterflies. Together with the plants on which they feed* (London, 1766).

11 Masayasu Konishi and Yosiaki Itô, 'Early Entomology in East Asia', in *History of Entomology*, ed. Ray F. Smith, Thomas E. Mittler and Carroll N. Smith (Palo Alto, CA, 1973), pp. 1–21.

12 See William E. Conner, ed., *Tiger Moths and Woolly Bears: Behavior, Ecology, and Evolution of the Arctiidae* (New York, 2009). A recent taxonomic change has moved the Tiger Moths yet again to the new family Erebidae.

13 *The Divine Comedy of Dante Alighieri*, ed. and trans. Robert M. Durling, introduction and notes Robert M. Durling and Ronald L. Martinez (New York, 1996), vol. II, p. 165.

14 Ibid., p. 717.

15 Giovanni Papini, *La spia del mondo: Schegge di poesia e di esperienza* (Florence, 1955), p. 42. Translation for author by Carlotta Giustozzi.

16 See Malcolm Davies and Jeyaraney Kathirithamby, *Greek Insects* (London, 1986), p. 102.

17 Pliny the Elder, *Natural History Books VIII–XVI*, trans. H. Rackham [1940] (London, 2012), vol. II, p. 184.

18 David L. Wagner, *Caterpillars of Eastern North America* (Princeton, NJ, 2005).

19 Ibid.

20 Malcolm J. Scoble, *The Lepidoptera: Form, Function and Diversity* (New York, 1992).

21 Wagner, *Caterpillars of Eastern North America*, p. 13.

22 Michael F. Land, 'Eyes and Vision', in *Encyclopedia of Insects*, ed. Vincent H. Resh and Ring T. Cardé, 2nd edn (London, 2009), p. 353; and Doekele G. Stavenga, 'Pseudopupils of Compound Eyes', in *Comparative Physiology and Evolution of Vision in Invertebrates*, ed. H. Autrum (New York, 1979), p. 382.

23 William E. Conner, Nickolay I. Hristov and Jesse R. Barber, 'Sound Strategies: Acoustic Aposematism, Startle, and Sonar Jamming', in *Tiger Moths and Woolly Bears*, pp. 177–92.

24 Jean-Henri Fabre, *The Fascinating Insect World*, ed. Edwin Way Teale, trans. Alexander Teixeira de Mattos (New York, 1956 [1901]), p. 84.

25 Philip S. Callahan, 'Moth and Candle: The Candle Flame as a Sexual Mimic of the Coded Infrared Wavelengths from a Moth Sex Scent (Pheromone)', *Applied Optics*, XVI/12 (1977), pp. 3089–97.

26 Wilson, *The Diversity of Life*, p. 51.

27 See Niels P. Kristensen and Andrzej W. Skalski, 'Phylogeny and Palaeontology', in *Handbuch der Zoologie / Handbook of Zoology*, ed. Niels P. Kristensen, vol. IV, part 35 (Berlin, 1999), pp. 7–15; David Penney and James E. Jepson, *Fossil Insects: An Introduction to Palaeoentomology* (Manchester, 2014).

28 C. C. Labandeira et al., 'Ninety-seven Million Years of Angiosperm–Insect Association: Paleobiological Insights into the Meaning of Coevolution', *Proceedings of the National Academy of Sciences*, XCI (1994), pp. 12278–82.

29 Gunnar Brehm et al., 'Montane Andean Rain Forests are a Global Diversity Hotspot of Geometrid Moths', *Journal of Biogeography*, XXII (2005), pp. 1621–7.

30 J. B. Heppner, 'Faunal Regions and the Diversity of Lepidoptera', *Tropical Lepidoptera*, II (1991) (suppl. 1), pp. 1–85.

31 See Scoble, *The Lepidoptera*.

32 Wagner, *Caterpillars of Eastern North America*, p. 13.

33 See Roy Leverton, *Enjoying Moths* (London, 2001).

34 See Theodore D. Sargent, *Legion of the Night: The Underwing Moths* (Philadelphia, PA, 1976).

35 Other phoretic ('hitching a ride') species include those discovered living on spiny pocket mice in Costa Rica.

36 Jan C. Axmacher et al., 'Diversity of Geometrid Moths (Lepidoptera: Geometridae) along an Afrotropical Elevational Rainforest Transect', *Diversity and Distributions*, X (2004), pp. 293–302.

37 See, for example, Takashi Kohyama, 'Size-structured Tree Populations in Gap-Dynamic Forest – The Forest Architecture Hypothesis for the Stable Coexistence of Species', *Journal of Ecology*, LXXXI (1993), pp. 131–43.

38 Wilson, *The Diversity of Life*.

39 See S. R. Bucheli, J. A. Bytheway and D. A. Gangitano, 'Necrophagous Caterpillars Provide Human mtDNA Evidence', *Journal of Forensic Sciences*, LV (2010), pp. 1130–32.

40 Michael Majerus, *Moths* (London, 2002).

41 Yeo Jin, *Pine Caterpillar Moths That Ate Oak Leaves* (갈잎 먹은 송충이들) (Seoul, 1987).

42 Jeffrey S. Dukes et al., 'Responses of Insect Pests, Pathogens, and Invasive Plant Species to Climate Change in the Forests of Northeastern North America', *Canadian Journal of Forest Research*, XXXIX (2009), pp. 231–48.

43 Butterfly Conservation, *The State of Britain's Larger Moths 2013* (Wareham, 2013).

44 F. Szentkirályi, 'Fifty-year-long Insect Survey in Hungary: T. Jermy's Contributions to Light Trapping', *Acta Zoologica Academiae Scientiarum Hungaricae*, XLVIII/1 (2002), pp. 85–105.

45 Jennifer Owen, *Wildlife of a Garden: A Thirty-year Study* (Peterborough, 2010).

46 Dave Goulson, *A Buzz in the Meadow* (London, 2014).

47 See Ilka Hanski, 'Metapopulation Dynamics', *Nature*, CCCXCVI (5 November 1998), pp. 41–9.

48 Dave Goulson, 'Neonicotinoids and Bees: What's all the Buzz?', *Significance*, X (June 2013), pp. 6–11.

49 Christiaan Both et al., 'Climate Change and Population Declines in a Long-distance Migratory Bird', *Nature*, CDXLI (2006), pp. 81–3.

50 W. A. Haber and G. W. Franke, 'Pollination of Luehea (Tiliacea) in Costa Rican Deciduous Forest', *Ecology*, LXIII/6 (1982), pp. 1740–50.

51 Scoble, *The Lepidoptera*, p. 177.

52 J. Arditti et al., '"Good Heavens What Insect Can Suck it": Charles Darwin, *Angraecum sesquipedale* and *Xanthepan morganii praedicta*', *Botantical Journal of the Linnean Society*, CLXIX (2012), pp. 403–32.

53 See Jerry A. Powell, *Biological Interrelationships of Moths and Yucca schottii* (Berkeley, CA, 1984).

54 Scoble, *The Lepidoptera*, p. 182.

55 Paul Latham, 'Edible Caterpillars and their Food Plants in Bas Congo, Democratic Republic of Congo', *African Botanic Gardens Network Bulletin*, III/3 (1999).

56 Wagner, *Caterpillars of Eastern North America*, p. 9.

57 Scoble, *The Lepidoptera*.

58 Yunan Yang, et al., 'Silkworms Culture as a Source of Protein for Humans in Space', *Advances in Space Research*, XLIII (2009), pp. 1236–42.

59 See Claire Waterton, Rebecca Ellis and Brian Wynne, *Barcoding Nature: Shifting Cultures of Taxonomy in an Age of Biodiversity Loss* (London, 2013).

60 See Jeffrey C. Miller, Daniel H. Janzen and Winifred Hallwachs, *100 Butterflies and Moths: Portraits from the Tropical Forests of Costa Rica* (Cambridge, MA, 2007).

61 David Agassiz, '*Prays peregrina* sp. n. (Yponomeutidae) a Presumed Adventive Species in Greater London', *Nota Lepidopterologica*, XXX/2 (2007), pp. 407–10.

62 James A. Secord, 'The Crisis of Nature', in *Cultures of Nature*, ed. N. Jardine, J. A. Secord and E. C. Spary (Cambridge, 1996), pp. 447–59; Waterton et al., *Barcoding Nature*.

63 Daniel H. Janzen et al., 'Wedding Biodiversity Inventory of a Large and Complex Lepidoptera Fauna with DNA barcoding', *Philosophical Transactions: Biological Sciences*, CCCLX/1462 (2005), pp. 1835–45.

64 Axel Hausmann et al., 'Now DNA Barcoded: The Butterflies and Larger Moths of Germany', *Spixiana*, XXXIV/1 (2011), pp. 47–58.

65 Waterton et al., *Barcoding Nature*.

66 Stefan Helmreich, *Alien Ocean: Anthropological Voyages in Microbial Seas* (Berkeley, CA, 2009), p. 8.

1 Michel Foucault, *The Order of Things: An Archaeology of the Human Sciences* [1966] (Oxford, 2002), p. 144.

2 Cited in Michael Majerus, *Moths* (London, 2002), p. 11.

3 See Malcolm Davies and Jeyaraney Kathirithamby, *Greek Insects* (London, 1986).

4 Kjell B. Sandved and Jo Brewer, *Butterflies* (New York, 1976), p. 33.

5 Davies and Kathirithamby, *Greek Insects*; Günter Morge, 'Entomology in the Western World in Antiquity and in Medieval Times', in *History of Entomology*, ed. Ray F. Smith, Thomas E. Mittler and Carroll N. Smith (Palo Alto, CA, 1973), pp. 37–80.

6 Cited in Sandved and Brewer, *Butterflies*, p. 33.

7 Ibid.

8 Moses Harris, *The Aurelian or Natural History of English Insects: Namely, Moths and Butterflies. Together with the plants on which they feed* (London, 1766).

9 Benjamin Wilkes, *English Moths and Butterflies, Representing their Changes into the Caterpillar, Chrysalis, and Fly States, and the Plants, Flowers, and Fruits, whereon they Feed* [c. 1749], 3rd edn (Worthing, 1824).

10 Adrian Hardy Haworth, *Lepidoptera Britannica* (London, 1803), p. xxv.

11 Ibid.

12 Gabrielli Aldo, ed., *Grande dizionario italiano* (Milan, 2001–11).

13 Ibid.

14 Mary Schoeser, *Silk* (New Haven, CT, 2007).

15 Carl Linnaeus, *Systema naturae: per regna tria naturæ, secundum classes, ordines, genera, species, cum characteribus et differentiis*, 10th edn (Holmiæ [Stockholm], 1758).

16 Carl Alexander Clerck, *Icones insectorum rariorum cum nominibus eorum trivialibus locisque e C. Linnaeus syst. nat. allegatis* (Stockholm, 1759–64); Nikolaus Poda von Neuhaus, *Insecta Musei Graecensis* (Vienna, 1761).

17 See Andrew Polaszek and Edward O. Wilson, 'Sense and Stability

in Animal Names', *Trends in Ecology and Evolution*, xx/8 (2005), pp. 421–2.

18 See Lisbet Koerner, 'Carl Linnaeus in his Time and Place', in *Cultures of Natural History*, ed. Nicholas Jardine, J. Anne Secord and Emma C. Spary (Cambridge, 1996), pp. 145–62.

19 Pliny the Elder, *Natural History Books VIII–XVI*, trans. H. Rackham (London, 2012 [1940]), vol. II, p. 184.

20 Thomas Moffet, *Insectorum sive minimorum animalium theatrum* (London, 1634).

21 A. Maitland Emmet, *The Scientific Names of the British Lepidoptera* (Colchester, 1991).

22 See Londa Schiebinger, 'Gender and Natural History', in *Cultures of Natural History*, ed. Jardine et al., pp. 163–77.

23 Emmet, *The Scientific Names of the British Lepidoptera*.

24 See Theodore D. Sargent, *Legion of the Night: The Underwing Moths* (Philadelphia, PA, 1976).

25 Schiebinger, 'Gender and Natural History'.

26 Dieter E. Zimmer, *A Guide to Nabokov's Butterflies and Moths* (Hamburg, 2001).

27 Dieter E. Zimmer, *Butterflies and Moths in Nabokov's Published Writings*, www.d-e-zimmer.de, accessed 12 December 2014.

28 Interview with Harrison Birtwistle cited in Rodney Lister, 'The Proms-Birtwistle, Gubaidulina, and More', *Sequenza 21 / The Contemporary Classical Music Community*, www. sequenza21.com, accessed 11 May 2014.

3 AURELIANS

1 Walter Benjamin, 'Unpacking my Collection: A Talk about Book Collecting' [1931], in *Illuminations*, ed. Hannah Arendt, trans. Harry Zohn (London, 1973), p. 67.

2 Darcy W. Thompson, 'Fauna', in *A Companion to Greek Studies*, ed. Leonard Whibley (Cambridge, 1906), pp. 34–51.

3 Pliny the Elder, *Natural History Books VIII–XVI*, trans. H. Rackham (London, 2012 [1940]), vol. II, p. 159.

4 See Günter Morge, 'Entomology in the Western World in Antiquity and in Medieval Times', in *History of Entomology*, ed. Ray F. Smith, Thomas E. Mittler and Carroll N. Smith (Palo Alto, CA, 1973), pp. 37–80.

5 See Paula Findlen, *Possessing Nature: Museums, Collecting, and Scientific Culture in Early Modern Italy* (Berkeley, CA, 1994).

6 Brian G. Ogilvie, *The Science of Describing: Natural History in Renaissance Europe* (Chicago, IL, 2005).

7 Ulisse Aldrovandi, *De animalibus insectis libri septem* (Bologna, 1602).

8 Thomas Moffet, *Insectorum sive minimorum animalium theatrum* (London, 1634).

9 A. Maitland Emmet, *The Scientific Names of the British Lepidoptera* (Colchester, 1991), p. 15.

10 Jan Swammerdam, *Historia insectorum generalis* (Utrecht, 1669). See also Max Beier, 'The Early Naturalists and Anatomists During the Renaissance and Seventeenth Century', in *History of Entomology*, ed. Smith et al., pp. 81–94.

11 Matthew Cobb, 'Malpighi, Swammerdam and the Colourful Silkworm: Replication and Visual Reproduction in Early Modern Science', *Annals of Science*, LIX (2002), pp. 111–47.

12 René-Antoine Ferchault de Réaumur, *Mémoires pour servir à l'histoire des insectes* [1734] (Amsterdam, 1737–41).

13 See Mary Terrall, *Catching Nature in the Act: Réaumur and the Practice of Natural History in the Eighteenth Century* (Chicago, IL, 2014).

14 Charles De Geer, *Mémoires pour servir à l'histoire des insectes* (Stockholm, 1752–78).

15 John Ray, *The Wisdom of God in the Works of the Creation* [1691] (London, 2005).

16 Moses Harris, *The Aurelian or Natural History of English Insects: Namely, Moths and Butterflies. Together with the plants on which they feed* (London, 1766).

17 David Grimaldi, 'Moses Harris: Naturalist and Artist', in *Natural Histories: Extraordinary Rare Book Selections from the American*

Museum of Natural History Library, ed. Tom Baione (New York, 2012), pp. 48–51.

18 Moses Harris, *The Aurelian's Pocket Companion* (London, 1775).

19 Adrian Hardy Haworth, *Lepidoptera Britannica* (London, 1803), p. xiv.

20 Ibid.

21 Findlen, *Possessing Nature*.

22 Kathleen S. Murphy, 'Collecting Slave Traders: James Petiver, Natural History, and the British Slave Trade', *William and Mary Quarterly*, LXX/4 (2013), p. 640.

23 Murphy, 'Collecting Slave Traders', pp. 639, 648, 651.

24 Ibid., p. 659.

25 Findlen, *Possessing Nature*.

26 Michael Dettelbach, 'Humboldtian Science', in *Cultures of Natural History*, ed. Nicholas Jardine, Anne Secord and Emma C. Spary (Cambridge, 1996), pp. 287–384.

27 Natalie Zemon Davis, *Women on the Margins: Three Seventeenth-century Lives* (Cambridge, MA, 1995).

28 Paula Schrynemakers, 'Made Merian', in *Natural Histories: Extraordinary Rare Book Selections from the American Museum of Natural History Library*, ed. Tom Baione (New York, 2012), pp. 24–7.

29 See Janice Neri, *The Insect and the Image: Visualizing Nature in Early Modern Europe, 1500–1700* (Minneapolis, MN, 2011).

30 James S. Miller, 'The Volumes of Cramer and Stoll: A Timeless Contribution to the Science of Butterflies and Moths', in *Natural Histories*, ed. Baione, pp. 57–60.

31 Ioannis Antonii Scopoli, *Entomologia carniolica, exhibens insecta carnoliæ indigena et distributa in ordines, genera, species, varietates methodo Linneana* (Vienna, 1763).

32 Michael Denis and Ignaz Schiffermüller, *Ankündung eines systematischen Werkes von den Schmetterlingen der Wienergegend* (Vienna, 1775)

33 Carl H. Lindroth, 'Systematics Specializes Between Fabricius and Darwin: 1800–1859', in *History of Entomology*, ed. Smith et al., pp. 119–54.

34 See John F. McDiarmid Clark, *Bugs and the Victorians* (New Haven, CT, 2009).

35 Gottlieb August Wilhelm Herrich-Schäffer, *Systematische Bearbeitung der Schmetterlinge von Europa, zugleich als Text, Revision, und Supplement zu Jakob Hübners Sammlung Europäischer Schmetterlinge*, vols I–VI (Regensburg, 1843–56).

36 W. Conner Sorensen, *Brethren of the Net: American Entomology, 1840–1880* (Tuscaloosa, AL, 1995).

37 Cited in Theodore D. Sargent, *Legion of the Night: The Underwing Moths* (Philadelphia, PA, 1976), p. 9.

38 Ibid.

39 H. G. Wells, 'The Moth' [1895], in *The Short Stories of H. G. Wells* (London, 1927), pp. 302–12.

40 Ibid., pp. 304, 307, 312.

41 See J. C. Melvill, 'A Sketch of Kersall Moor, with Special Allusion to the Discovery there of *Oecophora woodiella* Curtis', *Lancashire and Cheshire Naturalist*, CLXI (1924), pp. 207–12.

42 P.B.M. Allan, 'The Kentish Buccaneers', in *Talking of Moths* (Newtown, 1943).

43 James Francis Stephens cited in Richard South, *The Moths of the British Isles*, ed. H. M. Edelstein and D. S. Fletcher (London, 1961 [1907]), vol. I, pp. 314–15.

44 Allan cited in Sargent, *Legion of the Night*, p. 107.

45 Vladimir Nabokov, *Speak, Memory* [1951] (London, 1969), p. 107.

46 McDunnough cited in Dieter E. Zimmer, *Butterflies and Moths in Nabokov's Published Writings*, www.d-e-zimmer.de, accessed 12 December 2014.

47 Letter from Nabokov to Glenn Collins, 20 August 1975, in Brian Boyd and Robert Michael Pyle, eds, *Nabokov's Butterflies: Published and Unpublished Writings* (Boston, MA, 2000), p. 717.

48 Harris, *The Aurelian or Natural History of English Insects*.

49 Walter Benjamin, 'Butterfly Hunt', in *Walter Benjamin: Selected Writings*, vol. III: *1935–1938*, ed. Marcus Paul Bullock and Michael William Jennings (Cambridge, MA, 2003), p. 351.

50 Benjamin, 'Unpacking my Collection', p. 60.

51 See Findlen, *Possessing Nature*.

4 DRAWN TO THE FLAME

1 Proverb translated by Carlotta Giustozzi.

2 Cited in Theodore D. Sargent, *Legion of the Night: The Underwing Moths* (Philadelphia, PA, 1976), p. 95.

3 Sheikh Muslih-uddin Sa'di Shirazi (Sa'di of Shiraz), *The Gulistan (The Rose Garden)*, trans. Edward Eastwick (London, 2000 [1259]).

4 Sabine Rewald, *Balthus* (New York, 1984), p. 51.

5 Johann Wolfgang von Goethe, 'Ecstatic Longing' [*Selige Sehnsucht*, 1814], in *Selected Poetry*, trans. David Luke (London, 1999), p. 183.

6 Goethe, *Selected Poetry*, p. 268.

7 Kahlil Gibran, *Broken Wings: A Novel* [1912] (London, 1998).

8 James Thurber, *Fables for Our Time and Famous Poems Illustrated* (New York, 1940).

9 Cyprian Ekwensi, *People of the City* [1954] (London, 1963), p. 5.

10 Jean Rhys, *Wide Sargasso Sea* (Harmondsworth, 1966), p. 67.

11 Ibid., p. 67–8.

12 Ibid., p. 68.

13 Karl Marx, 'Notebooks on Epicurean Philosophy', in Karl Marx / Frederick Engels, *Collected Works* (London, 1975 [1835–43]), vol. I, p. 492.

14 George E. McCarthy, *Marx and Aristotle: Nineteenth-century German Social Theory and Classical Antiquity* (Savage, MD, 1992).

15 Sonia Hirt, *Iron Curtains: Gates, Suburbs and Privatization of Space in the Post-Socialist City* (Chichester, 2012).

16 Bessatsu taiyō, 速水御舟: 日本画を「破壊」する／[別冊太陽編集部編] (*Hayami gyoshū: nihonga o hakai suru*) (Tokyo, 2009).

17 See Philip S. Callahan, 'Moth and Candle: The Candle Flame as a Sexual Mimic of the Coded Infrared Wavelengths from a Moth Sex Scent (Pheromone)', *Applied Optics*, XVI/12 (1977), pp. 3089–97.

18 Henry S. Hsiao, *Attraction of Moths to Light and to Infrared Radiation* (San Francisco, CA, 1972).

19 See Natalie Wolchover, 'Why are Moths Drawn to Artificial Lights?', *Livescience* (25 March 2011), www.livescience.com.

20 Callahan, 'Moth and Candle', p. 3089.

21 Ibid., p. 3097.

22 Wolchover, 'Why are Moths Drawn to Artificial Lights?'.

23 Hsiao, *Attraction of Moths to Light and to Infrared Radiation*, p. 35.

24 Ibid.

25 See, for example, Axel Hausmann, 'Untersuchungen zum Massensterben von Nachtfaltern an Industriebeleuchtungen', *Atlanta*, XXIII/3–4 (1992), pp. 411–16; T. Longcore and C. Rich, 'Ecological Light Pollution', *Frontiers in Ecology and the Environment*, II/4 (2004), pp. 191–8.

26 See Axel Hausmann, 'Introduction', in *The Geometrid Moths of Europe: vol I* (Vester Skerninge, 2001), pp. 13–77.

27 Adrian Woodruffe-Peacock, 'Broughton Woods', in *Lincolnshire Naturalists Union* (1905), vol. I, p. 173.

28 Kathy Marks, 'Australia's Bogong Moth Invasion Turns Even Yawning into a Potential Health Hazard', *The Independent* (4 November 2013).

29 Stan Brakhage, *By Brakhage: An Anthology, Volume I*, interview in 2002 with Bruce Kawin (Criterion Collection, DVD).

5 VISITATIONS

1 Donald Culross Peattie cited in Theodore D. Sargent, *Legion of the Night: The Underwing Moths* (Philadelphia, PA, 1976), p. 1.

2 Carlos R. Beutelspacher, *Las Mariposas entre los antiguos mexicanos* (Mexico City, 1988); George Kubler, 'The Iconography of the Art of Teotihuacán', *Studies in Pre-Columbian Art and Archaeology*, IV (1967), pp. 1–40.

3 Kjell B. Sandved and Jo Brewer, *Butterflies* (New York, 1976), p. 41.

4 See Svetlana Alpers, *The Art of Describing: Dutch Art in the Seventeenth Century* (Chicago, IL, 1983); and Janice Neri, *The Insect*

and the Image: Visualizing Nature in Early Modern Europe, 1500–1700 (Minneapolis, MN, 2011).

5 Cited ibid.

6 Michael Majerus, *Moths* (London, 2002), p. 17. See www.norfolk-wildlifetrust.org.uk for more information on the Ghost Moth.

7 Durga Chew-Bose, 'Andrea Arnold in Brontë Country', interview with Andrea Arnold in www.interviewmagazine.com, accessed 6 August 2014.

8 Virginia Woolf, 'The Death of the Moth' [1919], in *The Death of the Moth and Other Essays* (London, 1942), p. 9.

9 Virginia Woolf, 'Reading' [1919], in *Collected Essays: Volume II* (London, 1966), pp. 12–33.

10 Virginia Woolf, *To the Lighthouse* [1927] (Oxford, 2000), p. 183.

11 Woolf, 'Reading', p. 22.

12 Ibid.

13 Ibid., p. 23.

14 Ibid.

15 Ibid., p. 25.

16 Woolf, 'The Death of the Moth', p. 11.

17 Ibid.

18 Francis Orpen Morris, *A Natural History of British Moths* (London, 1871). On the role of natural history in Woolf's writing, see Christina Alt, *Virginia Woolf and the Study of Nature* (Cambridge, 2010); and Harvena Richter, 'Hunting the Moth: Virginia Woolf and the Creative Imagination', in *Virginia Woolf: Revaluation and Continuity*, ed. Ralph Freedman (Berkeley, CA, 1980), pp. 13–28.

19 Virginia Woolf, *The Waves* [1931] (London, 2000), p. 10.

20 Virginia Woolf, *Jacob's Room* [1922] (Oxford, 1992), p. 61.

21 Ulrich von Bülow, Heike Gfrereis and Ellen Strittmatter, *Wandernde Schatten: W. G. Sebalds Unterwelt* (Marbach am Neckar, 2008).

22 W. G. Sebald, *Austerlitz*, trans. Anthea Bell [2001] (London, 2002), p. 131.

23 W. G. Sebald, interviewed on BBC Radio 3, *Night Waves* (5 October 2001), available from the British Library.

24 Sebald, *Austerlitz*, p. 127.
25 Ibid., pp. 132, 134.
26 Ibid., p. 408.
27 Norman Riley, *Some British Moths* (London, 1944), p. 9.
28 Majerus, *Moths*, p. 18; Riley, *Some British Moths*, p. 9.
29 John Keats, 'Ode on Melancholy' [1819], in *Selected Poems*, intro. John Barnard (London, 2007), p. 195.
30 Edgar Allan Poe, 'The Sphinx' [1846], in *The Complete Tales and Poems* (London, 1982), pp. 471–4.
31 John Duncan Macmillan, 'Holman Hunt's *Hireling Shepherd*: Some Reflections on a Victorian Pastoral', *Art Bulletin*, LIV/2 (1972), pp. 187–97.
32 'Sfinge testa di morto', www.farfalledalmondo.it, accessed 12 December 2014.
33 Interview with Carlos Amorales to accompany the exhibition 'Order, Chaos, and the Space Between', held at the Steele Gallery, Phoenix Art Museum (Off Madison Ave Films, 2013), available at http://vimeo.com.
34 'Hastings and St Leonard's Moth Project', graffoto1.blogspot.de, accessed 15 December 2014.

6 ANY COLOUR YOU LIKE

1 John Keats, 'The Eve of St Agnes' [1819], in *The Complete Poetical Works and Letters of John Keats*, ed. H. E. Scudder (Boston, 1889), p. 131.
2 Nicole Reynolds, *Building Romanticism: Literature and Architecture in Nineteenth-century Britain* (Ann Arbor, MI, 2010), p. 25.
3 Lorraine Daston and Peter Galison, *Objectivity* (New York, 2007), p. 415.
4 See A. D. Briscoe, 'Molecular Diversity of Visual Pigments in the Butterfly *Papilio glaucus*', *Naturwissenschaften*, LXXXV (1998), pp. 33–5; and L. Chitka, 'Does Bee Colour Vision Predate the Evolution of Flower Colour?', *Naturwissenschaften*, LXXXIII (1996), pp. 136–8.

5 David Grimaldi, 'Moses Harris: Naturalist and Artist', in *Natural Histories: Extraordinary Rare Book Selections from the American Museum of Natural History Library*, ed. Tom Baione (New York, 2012), pp. 48–51.

6 On the different 'registers' of colour, see, for example, Julia Kristeva, *Desire in Language* [1972] (Berkeley, CA, 1980).

7 Kjell B. Sandved and Jo Brewer, *Butterflies* (New York, 1976).

8 Malcolm Scoble, *The Lepidoptera: Form, Function, and Diversity*.

9 Ibid.

10 Sandved and Brewer, *Butterflies*.

11 Philip Ball, *The Self-made Tapestry: Pattern Formation in Nature* (Oxford, 1999), p. 99.

12 See, for example, Robert J. Richards, *The Tragic Sense of Life: Ernst Haeckel and the Struggle over Evolutionary Thought* (Chicago, IL, 2008).

13 Allen Carlson, 'Nature, Aesthetic Appreciation, and Knowledge', *Journal of Aesthetics and Art Criticism*, LIII/4 (1995), pp. 393–400.

14 Stephen Jay Gould, 'No Science Without Fancy, No Art Without Facts', in *I Have Landed: Splashes and Reflections in Natural History* (London, 2003), pp. 29–53.

15 Edward O. Wilson, *Biophilia* (Cambridge, MA, 1984).

16 Stan Brakhage, 'Metaphors on Vision', *Film Culture*, XXX (1963), cited in *Colour*, ed. David Batchelor (Cambridge, MA, 2008), p. 145.

7 PRETENDERS

1 Vladimir Nabokov, *The Gift* (London, 1981 [1963]), p. 105.

2 David L. Wagner, *Caterpillars of Eastern North America* (Princeton, NJ, 2005).

3 Norman Riley, *Some British Moths* (London, 1944).

4 Wagner, *Caterpillars of Eastern North America*, pp. 22, 24.

5 Michael Majerus, *Moths* (London, 2002), p. 178.

6 Henri Bergson, *Creative Evolution*, trans. Arthur Mitchell (Mineola, NY, 1998 [1907]), pp. 173–4.

7 See also Hugh Raffles, *Insectopedia* (New York, 2010).

8 Wagner, *Caterpillars of Eastern North America*.

9 M. S. Singer, K. C. Mace and E. A. Bernays, 'Self-Medication as Adaptive Plasticity: Increased Ingestion of Plant Toxins by Parasitized Caterpillars', *plos one*, iv/3 (2009).

10 Wagner, *Caterpillars of Eastern North America*, p. 179.

11 Ibid., p. 198.

12 Ibid., p. 200.

13 Ibid., p. 224.

14 Ibid., p. 305.

15 Ibid.

16 J. E. Barber and William E. Conner, 'Tiger Moth Jams Bat Sonar', *Science*, cccxxv (2009), pp. 325–7.

17 William E. Conner, Nickolay I. Hristov and Jesse R. Barber, 'Sound Strategies: Acoustic Aposematism, Startle, and Sonar Jamming', in *Tiger Moths and Woolly Bears: Behaviour, Ecology, and Evolution of the Arctiidae*, ed. William E. Conner (New York, 2009), pp. 177–92.

18 Miriam Rothschild, 'British Aposematic Lepidoptera', in John Heath and A. Maitland Emmet, *The Moths and Butterflies of Great Britain and Ireland* (Colchester, 1985), vol. ii, pp. 9–62.

19 Theodore D. Sargent, *Legion of the Night: The Underwing Moths* (Philadelphia, pa, 1976), p. 147.

20 Ibid., p. 181.

21 Michael Majerus, *Melanism: Evolution in Action* (Oxford, 1998).

22 Graeme D. Ruxton, Thomas N. Sherratt and Michael P. Speed, *Avoiding Attack: The Evolutionary Ecology of Crypsis, Warning Signals, and Mimicry* (Oxford, 2004), p. 10.

23 Theodore D. Sargent, 'Behavioural Adaptations of Cryptic Moths', *Animal Behaviour*, xvii/4 (1969), pp. 670–72.

24 Judith Hooper, *Of Moths and Men: Intrigue, Tragedy, and the Peppered Moth* (London, 2002).

25 Jaape de Roode, 'The Moths of War', *New Scientist*, cxcvi (8 December 2007).

26 L. M. Cook et al., 'Selective Bird Predation on the Peppered Moth: The Last Experiment of Michael Majerus', *Biology Letters*, viii (2012), pp. 609–12.

27 Malcolm J. Scoble, *The Lepidoptera*: *Form, Function and Diversity* (New York, 1992).

28 Jadranka Rota and David L. Wagner, 'Predator Mimicry: Metalmark Moths Mimic Their Jumping Spider Predators', PLOS ONE, I/1 (2006).

29 Ruxton, Sherratt and Speed, *Avoiding Attack,* p. 164.

30 Vladimir Nabokov, *Speak, Memory* [1951] (London, 1969), p. 98.

31 Ibid.

32 See Brian Boyd, *Vladimir Nabokov: The American Years* (Princeton, NJ, 1991).

33 See also Stephen Jay Gould, 'No Science Without Fancy, No Art Without Facts', in *I Have Landed: Splashes and Reflections in Natural History* (London, 2003); Charles Lee Remington, 'Lepidoptera Studies', in *The Garland Companion to Vladimir Nabokov*, ed. Vladimir E. Alexandrov (New York, 1995), pp. 274–83.

34 Roger Caillois, 'Mimicry and Legendary Psychasthenia', trans. John Shepley, *October*, XXXI (Winter 1984), pp. 16–32.

35 Ibid., p. 22.

36 See Lucien Cuénot, *Les Moyens de défense dans la série animale* (Paris, 1892).

37 Caillois, 'Mimicry and Legendary Psychasthenia', p. 23.

38 Ibid., p. 25.

39 Ibid., p. 27.

40 See, for example, Stephen Jay Gould and Niles Eldredge, 'Punctuated Equilibria: The Tempo and Mode of Evolution Reconsidered', *Paleobiology*, III (1977), pp. 115–51.

8 SPINNERS AND MONSTERS

1 Cited in Jon R. Stone, ed., *Routledge Book of World Proverbs* (Oxford, 2006), p. 320.

2 Charles Butler cited in Erika Mae Olbricht, 'Made Without Hands: The Representation of Labor in Early Modern Silkworm and Beekeeping Manuals', in *Insect Poetics*, ed. Eric C. Brown (Minneapolis, MN, 2006), p. 223.

3 Bruno Marcandalli, 'The Science of Silk', in Mary Schoeser, *Silk* (New Haven, CT, 2007), pp. 232–43.

4 Ibid, pp. 232–3.

5 Ibid, p. 22.

6 Ibid, p. 18.

7 See Tadao Yokoyama, 'The History of Sericultural Science in Relation to Industry', in *History of Entomology*, ed. Ray F. Smith, Thomas E. Mittler and Carroll N. Smith (Palo Alto, CA, 1973), pp. 267–84.

8 J. Thorley, 'The Silk Trade between China and the Roman Empire at its Height, Circa AD 90–130', *Greece and Rome*, 2nd series, XVIII/1 (1971), pp. 71–80.

9 Susan Whitfield, *Life along the Silk Road* (London, 1999), p. 21.

10 Susan Meller, *Silk and Cotton: Textiles from the Central Asia That Was* (New York, 2013).

11 Schoeser, *Silk*, pp. 24–6.

12 Whitfield, *Life along the Silk Road*, p. 30.

13 Schoeser, *Silk*.

14 Ibid.

15 Luca Molà, *The Silk Industry of Renaissance Venice* (Baltimore, MD, 2000).

16 Schoeser, *Silk*, p. 49.

17 Ibid.

18 Olbricht, 'Made Without Hands', p. 236.

19 John Feltwell, *The Story of Silk* (Stroud, 1990), p. 47.

20 Moses Harris, *The Aurelian or Natural History of English Insects: Namely, Moths and Butterflies. Together with the plants on which they feed* (London, 1766), p. 41.

21 Olbricht, 'Made Without Hands' p. 228.

22 See Victor Houliston, 'Introduction', in Thomas Moffet, *The Silkewormes and their Flies* [1599] (Binghamton, NY, 1989).

23 Olbricht, 'Made Without Hands', p. 234.

24 Ibid.

25 Cited in Schoeser, *Silk*, p. 27.

26 W. G. Sebald, *The Rings of Saturn* [1995], trans. Michael Hulse (London, 2002), p. 282.

27 Cited in Olbricht, 'Made Without Hands", p. 233.

28 See, for example, Janet Browne, 'Biogeography and Empire', in *Cultures of Natural History*, ed. Nicholas Jardine, Anne Secord and Emma C. Spary (Cambridge, 1996), pp. 305–21.

29 Feltwell, *The Story of Silk*.

30 Yokoyama, 'The History of Sericultural Science in Relation to Industry'.

31 Ono Shuntaro, *Intellectual History of Mothra (Kodansha Gendaishinsho)* (Tokyo, 2007).

32 Ibid.

33 Yoshikuni Igarashi, 'Mothra's Gigantic Egg: Consuming the South Pacific in 1960s Japan', in *In Godzilla's Footsteps: Japanese Pop Culture Icons on the Global Stage*, ed. William M. Tsutsui and Michiko Ito (New York, 2006), p. 84.

34 See through-the-sapphire-sky.blogspot.de/2011/02/mothra-queen-moth-legacy-from-silk.html, accessed 6 August 2014.

35 Igarashi, 'Mothra's Gigantic Egg', p. 85.

36 This striking image is used by Igarashi. See also Simon Partner, *Assembled in Japan: Electrical Goods and the Making of the Japanese Consumer* (Berkeley, CA, 1999).

37 Zhu Zhu, 'Liang Shaoji: I, the Silkworm', in *Art of Change: New Directions from China*, ed. Stephanie Rosenthal (London, 2012), pp. 54–7.

Select Bibliography

GENERAL SOURCES

Aldrovandi, U., *De animalibus insectis libri septem* (Bologna, 1602)

Arditti, J., et al. '"Good Heavens what Insect can Suck it": Charles Darwin, *Angraecum sesquipedale* and *Xanthopan morganii praedicta*', *Botanical Journal of the Linnean Society* (2012), pp. 403–32

Baione, T., ed., *Natural Histories: Extraordinary Rare Book Selections from the American Museum of Natural History Library* (New York, 2012)

Ball, P., *The Self-made Tapestry: Pattern Formation in Nature* (Oxford, 1999)

Barber, J. E. and W. E. Conner, 'Tiger Moth Jams Bat Sonar', *Science*, cccxxv (2009), pp. 325–7

Boisduval, J. P., *Histoire naturelle des Insectes: species général des Lépidoptères* (Paris, 1836)

Brehm, G., et al., 'Montane Andean Rain Forests are a Global Diversity Hotspot of Geometrid Moths', *Journal of Biogeography*, xxxii (2005), pp. 1621–7

Brown, E. C., ed., *Insect Poetics* (Minneapolis, MN, 2006)

Clark, J.F.M., *Bugs and the Victorians* (New Haven, CT, 2009)

Clerck, C. A., *Icones insectorum rariorum cum nominibus eorum trivialibus locisque e C. Linnaeus syst. nat. allegatis* (Stockholm, 1759–64)

Cobb, M., 'Malpighi, Swammerdam and the Colourful Silkworm: Replication and Visual Reproduction in Early Modern Science', *Annals of Science*, LIX (2002), pp. 111–47

Conner, W. E., ed., *Tiger Moths and Woolly Bears: Behavior, Ecology, and Evolution of the Arctiidae* (New York, 2009)

Cook, L. M., et al., 'Selective Bird Predation on the Peppered Moth: The Last Experiment of Michael Majerus', *Biology Letters*, VIII (2012), pp. 609–12

De Geer, C., *Mémoires pour servir à l'histoire des insectes* (Stockholm, 1752–78)

de Roode, J., 'The Moths of War', *New Scientist*, CXCVI (8 December 2007)

Denis, M. and I. Schiffermüller, *Ankündung eines systematischen Werkes von den Schmetterlingen der Wienergegend* (Vienna, 1775)

Emmet, A. M., *The Scientific Names of the British Lepidoptera* (Colchester, 1991)

Fabre, J.–H., *The Fascinating Insect World*, ed. E. W. Teale, trans. A. Teixeira de Mattos (New York, 1956 [1901])

Findlen, P., *Possessing Nature: Museums, Collecting, and Scientific Culture in Early Modern Italy* (Berkeley, CA, 1994)

Gaston, K. J., 'The Magnitude of Global Insect Species Richness', *Conservation Biology*, V (1991), pp. 283–96

Gould, S. J., *I Have Landed: Splashes and Reflections in Natural History* (London, 2003)

Goulson, D., *A Buzz in the Meadow* (London, 2014)

Grimaldi, D., and M. S. Engel, *Evolution of the Insects* (Cambridge, 2005)

Hanski, I., 'Metapopulation Dynamics', *Nature*, CCCXCVI (5 November 1998), pp. 41–9

Harris, M., *The Aurelian or Natural History of English Insects: Namely, Moths and Butterflies. Together with the plants on which they feed* (London, 1766)

Haworth, A. H., *Lepidoptera Britannica* (London, 1803)

Heppner, J. B., 'Faunal Regions and the Diversity of Lepidoptera', *Tropical Lepidoptera*, II (1991) (supple. 1), pp. 1–85

Herrich-Schäffer, G.A.W., *Systematische Bearbeitung der Schmetterlinge von Europa, zugleich als Text, Revision, und Supplement zu Jakob Hübners Sammlung Europäischer Schmetterlinge*, I–VI (Regensburg, 1843–56)

Hooper, J., *Of Moths and Men: Intrigue, Tragedy, and the Peppered Moth* (London, 2002)

Hsiao, H. S., *Attraction of Moths to Light and to Infrared Radiation* (San Francisco, CA, 1972)

Janzen, D. H., et al., 'Wedding Biodiversity Inventory of a Large and Complex Lepidoptera Fauna with DNA barcoding', *Philosophical Transactions: Biological Sciences*, CCCVX/1462 (2005), pp. 1835–45

Jardine, N., J. A. Secord and E. C. Spary, eds, *Cultures of Natural History* (Cambridge, 1996), pp. 145–62

Kristensen, N. P., M. J. Scoble and O. Karsholt, 'Lepidoptera Phylogeny and Systematics: The State of Inventorying Moth and Butterfly Diversity', *Zootaxa*, MDCLXVIII (2007), pp. 699–747

Kukal, O. et al., 'Cold-induced Mitochondrial Degradation and Cryoprotectant Synthesis in Freeze-tolerant Arctic Caterpillars', *Journal of Comparative Physiology B*, CLVIII/6 (1989), pp. 661–71

Latreille, P. A., *Précis des caractères génériques des insectes, disposés dans un ordre naturel* (Bordeaux, 1796)

Leverton, R., *Enjoying Moths* (London, 2001)

Linnaeus, C., *Systema naturae: per regna tria naturæ, secundum classes, ordines, genera, species, cum characteribus et differentiis*, 10th edn (Holmiæ [Stockholm], 1758)

Majerus, M., *Moths* (London, 2002)

Melvill, J. C., 'A Sketch of Kersall Moor, with Special Allusion to the Discovery there of *Oecophora woodiella* Curtis', *Lancashire and Cheshire Naturalist*, CLXI (1924), pp. 207–12

Miller, J. C., D. H. Janzen and W. Hallwachs, *100 Butterflies and Moths: Portraits from the Tropical Forests of Costa Rica* (Cambridge, MA, 2007)

Moffet, T., *The Silkewormes and their Flies* (London, 1599)

—, *Insectorum sive minimorum animalium theatrum* (London, 1634)

Molà, L., *The Silk Industry of Renaissance Venice* (Baltimore, MD, 2000)

Montgomery, S. L., 'Carnivorous Caterpillars: The Behavior, Biogeography, and Conservation of Eupithecia (Lepidoptera: Geometridae) in the Hawaiian Islands', *GeoJournal*, VII/6 (1983), pp. 549–56

Murphy, K. S., 'Collecting Slave Traders: James Petiver, Natural History, and the British Slave Trade', *William and Mary Quarterly*, LXX/4 (2013), pp. 637–70

Neri, J., *The Insect and the Image: Visualizing Nature in Early Modern Europe, 1500–1700* (Minneapolis, MN, 2011)

Ogilvie, B. G., *The Science of Describing: Natural History in Renaissance Europe* (Chicago, IL, 2005)

Olbricht, E. A., 'Made Without Hands: The Representation of Labor in Early Modern Silkworm and Beekeeping Manuals', in *Insect Poetics*, ed. E. C. Brown (Minneapolis, MN, 2006)

Poda von Neuhaus, N., *Insecta musei graecensis* (Vienna, 1761)

Pogue, M. G., 'Biodiversity of Lepidoptera', in *Insect Biodiversity: Science and Society*, ed. R. G. Foottit and P. H. Adler (Oxford, 2009), pp. 325–55

Powell, J. A., *Biological Interrelationships of Moths and Yucca schottii* (Berkeley, CA, 1984)

Réaumur, R.–A.F. de, *Mémoires pour servir à l'histoire des insectes* (Amsterdam, 1734–42 [1734])

Richter, H., 'Hunting the Moth: Virginia Woolf and the Creative Imagination', in *Virginia Woolf: Revaluation and Continuity*, ed. R. Freeman (Berkeley, CA, 1980), pp. 13–28

Riley, N., *Some British Moths* (London, 1944)

Rothschild, M., 'British Aposematic Lepidoptera', in *The Moths and Butterflies of Great Britain and Ireland*, ed. John Heath and A. Maitland Emmet, vol. II (Colchester, 1985), pp. 9–62

Sargent, T. D., *Legion of the Night: The Underwing Moths* (Philadelphia, PA, 1976)

Schoeser, M., *Silk* (New Haven, CT, 2007)

Scoble, M. J., *The Lepidoptera: Form, Function, and Diversity* (New York, 1992)

Scopoli, I. A., *Entomologia carniolica, exhibens insecta carnoliae indigena et distributa in ordines, genera, species, varietates methodo Linneana* (Vienna, 1763)

Smith, R. F., T. E. Mittler and C. N. Smith, eds, *History of Entomology* (Palo Alto, CA, 1973)

Sorensen, W. C., *Brethren of the Net: American Entomology, 1840–1880* (Tuscaloosa, AL, 1995)

Swammerdam, J., *Historia insectorum generalis* (Utrecht, 1669)

Szentkirályi, F., 'Fifty-year-long Insect Survey in Hungary: T. Jermy's Contributions to Light Trapping', *Acta Zoologica Academiae Scientiarum Hungaricae*, XLVIII/1 (2002), pp. 85–105

Terrall, M., *Catching Nature in the Act: Réaumur and the Practice of Natural History in the Eighteenth Century* (Chicago, IL, 2014)

Wilkes, B., *English Moths and Butterflies, Representing their Changes into the Caterpillar, Chrysalis, and Fly States, and the Plants, Flowers, and Fruits, whereon they Feed* [*c.* 1749], 3rd edn (Worthing, 1824)

Woolf, V., 'The Death of the Moth' [1919], in *The Death of the Moth and Other Essays* (London, 1942)

Zeller, P. C., et al., *The Natural History of the Tineina* (London, 1855–73)

Zimmer, D. E., *A Guide to Nabokov's Butterflies and Moths* (Hamburg, 2001)

IDENTIFICATION GUIDES

Beadle, D., and S. Leckie, *Peterson Field Guide to Moths of Northeastern North America* (New York, 2012)

Holland, W. J., *The Moth Book: A Guide to the Moths of North America* (New York, 1968 [1903])

Manley, C., *British Moths*, 2nd edn (London, 2015)

Parenti, U., *A Guide to the Microlepidoptera of Europe* (Turin, 2000)

Powell, J. A., and P. A. Opler, *Moths of Western North America* (Berkeley, CA, 2009)

Redondo, V., J. Gastón and J. C. Vicente, *Las Mariposas de España Peninsular* (Zaragoza, 2010)

Robineau, R., *Guide des papillons nocturnes de France* (Paris, 2007)

Skinner, B., *Colour Identification Guide to Moths of the British Isles* (Stenstrup, 2009)

Sterling, P., and M. Parsons, *Field Guide to the Micro Moths of Great Britain and Ireland* (Gillingham, 2012)

Townsend, M., and P. Waring, *Concise Guide to the Moths of Great Britain and Ireland* (Gillingham, 2007)

Wagner, D. L., *Caterpillars of Eastern North America* (Princeton, NJ, 2005)

—, et al., *Owlet Caterpillars of Eastern North America* (Princeton, NJ, 2011)

Other excellent sources include the series on Japanese moths edited by Yasunori Kishida, the multi-volume *Moths of Europe* series by Patrice Leraut, the state-of-the-art series on European Geometridae edited by Axel Hausmann and others, and for Korea, 단행본, 한국 밤 곤충 도감 (Guide Book of Nocturnal Insects in Korea).

Associations and Websites

Amateur Entomologists' Society
www.amentsoc.org

British Entomological and Natural History Society
www.benhs.org.uk

Buglife – The Invertebrate Conservation Trust
www.buglife.org.uk

The Lepidopterists' Society
www.lepsoc.org

Sociedad Hispano-Luso-Americana de Lepidopterología (SHILAP)
www.redalyc.org

Societas Europaea Lepidopterologica
www.soceurlep.eu

Xerces Society for Invertebrate Conservation
www.xerces.org

Biodiversidad Virtual
www.biodiversidadvirtual.org

Biodiversity Heritage Library
www.biodiversitylibrary.org

Butterflies and Moths of North America
www.butterfliesandmoths.org

Les Carnets du Lépidoptériste Français
www.lepinet.fr

Digital Moths of Japan
www.jpmoth.org

Flemish Entomological Society / Vlaamse Vereniging voor
Entomologie
uahost.uantwerpen.be/vve

Forum Entomologici Italiani
www.entomologiitaliani.net

Lepidoptera Gallery
lepidopteragallery.org

Lépidoptères de France méridionale et de Corse
pathpiva.wifeo.com

The Lepidopterists' Society
www.lepsoc.org

Lepiforum
www.lepiforum.de
This site provides a wealth of images of European Lepidoptera and a discussion forum for help with identification

Lot Moths
www.lotmoths.com
This site is a comprehensive visual guide to moths from the Lot region of France

Moths and Butterflies of Europe and North Africa
www.leps.it

North American Moth Photographers Group
mothphotographersgroup.msstate.edu

Swedish Moths and Butterflies
www.lepidoptera.se

UK Moths
www.ukmoths.org.uk

Acknowledgements

My research for this book could not have been developed without the assistance, enthusiasm, expertise and generosity of many people. In particular I would like to thank David Agassiz, Jan Axmacher, Stephen Barber, Yasminah Beebeejaun, Ted Benton, Peter Buchner, Tony Butler, Alan Daws, Teresa Farino, Michael Flitner, Maria Gandy, Jörg Gelbrecht, Carlotta Giustozzi, Nick Greatorex-Davies, Axel Hausmann, James Hewson, Robin Howard, Sandra Jasper, Ole Karshott, Eje Kim, Gang-Li Kim, Paolo Mazzei, Wolfram Mey, Russell Miller, Miyuki Noguchi, Hyojin Pak, Richard Phillips, Victor Redondo, Jouko Veikkolainen, Pekka Veikkolainen, Colin Plant, Corinna Reetz, Martin Ritter, Jon Stokes, David L. Wagner, Karin Yabe, Zou Yi, Yue Zheng and Alberto Zilli. Thanks also to the staff at London's Natural History Museum, Berlin's Museum für Naturkunde and the British Library. I would also like to give special thanks to Kiera Chapman, who provided invaluable suggestions on the manuscript, and also to the series editor Jonathan Burt along with Harry Gilonis, Michael Leaman and Amy Salter at Reaktion for their perceptive comments and advice on different aspects of the production process. Finally, I must mention two recently departed denizens of the world of moths, Michael Fibiger and Umberto Parenti, for sharing their knowledge with me and many other moth enthusiasts.

Photo Acknowledgements

The author and publishers wish to express their thanks to the below sources of illustrative material and / or permission to reproduce it. Some locations are also given in the captions for the sake of brevity.

© ADAGP, Paris and DACS, London 2015: pp. 95, 136; photo Gerardo Aizpuru: p. 145 (top); photo courtesy Andreas Kay (www.flickr.com/andreaskay/albums): p. 25; photo Artothek, reproduced courtesy the Städel Museum, Frankfurt: p. 95; photos author: pp. 6, 8, 11, 13, 15, 20, 35, 43, 46, 53, 54, 55, 56, 99, 158 (foot), 165, 166; © Estate of Vanessa Bell, courtesy Henrietta Garnett: p. 113; courtesy Mike Beauregard: p. 28; BFI Southbank: p. 120 (top); Bibliothèque nationale de France, Paris: p. 106; courtesy Bildrechte Louis Busman, reproduced courtesy of the artist's estate: p. 86; Philippe Boissel: p. 167 (bottom); courtesy of the Estate of Stan Brakhage and Fred Camper (www.fredcamper.com): p. 101; photos British Library, London: pp. 132, 181, 185; photo Patricia Burkett: p. 150; photo J. S. Clark: p. 144 (top); DEA/Dani Jeske/Getty Images: p. 10; photo Mel Diotti: p. 169; reproduced courtesy K. A. Doktor-Sargent: p. 96; © Dumbarton Oaks Research Library and Collection Rare Books Collection: p. 76; photo © and courtesy fineArtImages: p. 22; Nick Garbutt/Barcroft Media/Getty Images: p. 135; Gemälde-galerie, Berlin (photo bpk/Gemäldegalerie, SMB/Jörg P. Anders): p. 107; courtesy Linden Gledhill: pp. 133, 134; portrait collection, Gripsholm Castle, Sweden: p. 49 (top right); © Philippe Halsman/Magnum Photos: p. 121; © The Heartfield Community of Heirs/VG Bild-Kunst, Bonn and DACS, London 2015: p. 120 (lower right); courtesy

John Horstman/itchydogimages: pp. 145 (foot), 159, 160; courtesy Adrian Hoskins: p. 26; reproduced courtesy the Estate of Faith Jaques: p. 92; Clinton Jenkins (Instituto de Pesquisas Ecológicas/ SavingSpecies): p. 24 (middle); photo courtesy Ivo Kindel: p. 29; courtesy Deborah Klein: p. 126; Luis Lara-Pérez: p. 27; photo Lynk Media: p. 149 top (this image is licensed under the Creative Commons Attribution-Share Alike 3.0 Unported license – readers are free to share – to copy, distribute and transmit the work, and to remix – to adapt the work – under the following conditions – you must attribute the work in the manner specified by the author or licensor (but not in any way that suggests that they endorse you or your use of the work) and – 'share alike' – if you alter, transform, or build upon this work, you may distribute the resulting work only under the same or similar license to this one); Peggy Macnamara Watercolors: p. 131; photo Manchester Galleries: p. 119; courtesy James Marsh: p. 124; photo Paolo Mazzei: p. 146 (top); from *Meyers Konverstions-Lexikon* (Leipzig, 1885–90) – photo Blibliographisches Institut, Leipzig: p. 175; photo Radek Mica/Getty Images: p. 14; Ministero per per i Beni e le Attività Culturali Soprintendenza Speciale per i Beni Archeologici di Napoli e Pompei / De Agostini Picture Library – Getty Images: p. 104; courtesy Airton Morassi: p. 155 (top); photo Daniel Morel: p. 34; photo Philippe Mothiron: p. 147; Natural History Museum, London: pp. 49 (left), 60, 61, 62, 63, 64, 67, 68, 71, 72, 73, 75, 79; Linda Nylind/Hayward Gallery, London: p. 193; Orion Pictures Corporation: p. 120 (lower left); courtesy Parham Elizabethan House: p. 187; Félix Pharand-Deschênes (Globaïa): p. 24 (middle); Rijks Museum, Amsterdam: p. 109; photo Jumpu Ronya, Itanagar, India: p. 176; Royal Collection Trust / © Her Majesty Queen Elizabeth II 2015: pp. 182–3; Sammlung Scharf-Gerstenberg, Stiftung Preußischer Kulturbesitz: pp. 120 lower right (photo © bpk – Bildagentur für Kunst, Kultur und Geschichte), 136; reproduced courtesy of Kjell B. Sandved: pp. 93, 137; photo Mark Snelson: p. 102; reproduced courtesy of the artist, copyright Maggie Taylor 2012: p. 57; photo courtesy Robert Thompson (Rothamsted Research): p. 156; © Joe Tilson, courtesy Marlborough Fine Art: p. 163; Toho Co., Ltd.: pp. 190, 191 ['Mothra vs. Godzilla' © 1964 Toho Co., Ltd. – 'Godzilla vs. Mothra' © 1924 Toho Co., Ltd. – GODZILLA, MOTHRA and The Character Designs and trademarks

Index